Nectar of Nondual Truth

CONTENTS

10 The Anatomy of Suffering
by Swami Brahmeshananda
With the knowledge of the nature of any given thing comes freedom. This fact would be especially welcome in the face of suffering, wherein locating its source by becoming aware of its dynamics would amount to its mastery and transcendence.

13 Madhu: The Sweet, Eternal Nectar
by Swami Sunirmalananda
The ancient rishis of India followed a well-conceived and expertly guided spiritual pathway which brought them to the discovery of a never-ending Bliss that they found lay behind all of phenomena.

14 The Immediacy of Consciousness
by Annapurna Sarada
Like intense concentration without end, but free of conceptualization, such is the thrilling description of pure Consciousness by the illumined seers of Mother India. It is the essence and the singular consistency of the Soul.

18 Dehypnotizing the Mind With Vedanta
by Anurag Neal Aronowitz
A religion that fulfils, a philosophy which clarifies all thought and conjecture — the Vedanta darshana accomplishes both for its fortunate adherents, beginning with clarification.

21 Nondual Polytheistic Plurality
by Lex Hixon
It would seem true, that even in the case of specialized paths which find their way into the highest reaches of insight and nonduality, that a taint of that old narrowness of perspective still haunts them. Unity still awaits.

23 The Embodied Practice of Shingon
by Rev. Kosho Finch
Relatively unknown in the pure religion of Buddhism is Shingon which, among other of its facets, deeply accents the participatory practice of pilgrimage to sacred spots.

29 The Roots of Suffering
by Anam Thubten Rinpoche
Both the roots and the removal of human suffering find light and clarity in this informative article designed to weaken the unripe human ego's hold while simultaneously fortifying practitioners to attain ultimate Freedom.

33 Beyond Intellectual Frame of Reference
by Babaji Bob Kindler
One major hurdle still keeps the clever, worldly-wise Western savant from gaining the "Peace that passes all understanding," or, attaining to that Freedom which transcends the intellectual frame of reference.

36 Christ: The Teacher in My Life
by Deacon Peter Solan
The personal relationship with the ideal form of God is a facet of religion that complements spiritual advancement, adding in the sweetness of divine love as it does.

38 Godblogs: Brahman Bytes
by Babaji Bob Kindler
Short but sedulous offerings designed to transmit needed daily spiritual sustenance to the aspiring soul.

40 The Political Ideal of Judaism
by Rabbi Rami Shapiro
Although the common complaint about politics throughout the ages has been injustice and all its unsavory concomitants, a few rare cultures have enjoyed a more refined system of government, such as that found laid out in the sacred scriptures of ancient Judaism.

44 The Motherhood of God
by O. P. Sharma
As exceptional a spiritual phenomenon as the Great Master Himself, is Sri Sarada Devi, His holy consort, only occasionally heralded even by sacred scripture. She is now seen as the Divine Mother incarnate. No citing of non-dual truth would be complete without Her.

48 The Fifty Eight Verses of the Encomium
by Babaji Bob Kindler

"...if the human being is divine by nature, as Swami Vivekananda reminded us of upon his arrival on the Western scene in 1893, and as Advaita Vedanta (nonduality) confirms in its wisdom scriptures through the pure minds and truthful lips of illumined seers such as he, then the remastery of the world and its powers should be a relatively simple matter..."

Publisher's Page

Sarada Ramakrishna Vivekananda – SRV Associations
"Setting the feet of humanity on the path of Universal Truth."

Notes on an Advaitic Journal

At the basis of Advaita as the philosophy of Shankara and his gurus, there is Advaita as experience. Advaita as experience represents that supreme place where all diversity merges in its Essence. It is not combatant or immiscible with qualified or dualistic approaches, but rather provides them their place of consummate arrival. Where actual practice rather than mere book learning is emphasized, where religion, philosophy and spirituality are not separate from one another, where knowledge and love, reason and devotion, are never divorced from each other, there does the truth of authentic nonduality effloresce.

Historically speaking, experiential Advaita originated with the ancient Rishis. Therefore, the Upanisads contain the nondual truths of the Vedas which declare: idam mahabhutam anantam aparam vijnanaghana eva, "This great Being is endless and without limit. It is a mass of indivisible Consciousness only."

SRV Associations & Universality

The SRV Associations are part of a worldwide movement of spiritual aspirants devoted to the study and practice of Vedanta and Divine Mother Wisdom. The ideals of this ancient pathway to God, exemplified in the lives of Sri Sarada Devi, Sri Ramakrishna and Swami Vivekananda, are the original and eternal perfection of the Soul and its inherent oneness with Reality, the manifesting of divinity in our lives, selfless service of all beings as God, and reverence for the ultimate unity of all sacred traditions. To this end our purpose is to study, worship, and contemplate Truth so that spirituality may flourish. This is the Advaitic way — "None else but Self, none other than Mother."

Nectar's Mission — Advaita-Satya-Amritam

In Sanskrit, amrita, nectar also means Immortality – and this is, indeed, what we are offering: opportunities to become aware of this Amrita that is our very Essence via the rarefied teachings from Vedanta and the World Religions and Philosophies that appear in each issue of Nectar.

Nectar of Non-Dual Truth is SRV Associations' heartfelt offering of highest Wisdom to the human community. It is the sincerest form of love and service we know to disseminate non-dual Truth and teachings which transmit pure knowledge, pure love, and true universality. Through Nectar we are working out SRV's mission of spiritual upliftment and education. Please join us; this is a universal movement.

Keeping Nectar in Print
Subscribe to Nectar of Non-Dual Truth

Nectar of Nondual Truth, or *Advaitasatyamrita* in Sanskrit, is a subscription-based instrument of Universal Religious & Philosophical Teachings. It requires subscriptions to stay in print. Please subscribe to Nectar using the form at the back of this issue.

You Can Help Others Receive Nectar

We continue to supply free copies to prison inmates, religious organizations, and low income persons in the U.S. You can help bridge the financial gap with a separate donation to Nectar. SRV Associations is a 501(c)3 tax-exempt organization.

To donate online, Visit: www.srv.org > Giving. To donate by check, mail to: SRV Associations, PO Box 1364, Honokaa, HI 96727 (payable to: SRV Associations)

808-990-3354 | srvinfo@srv.org | www.srv.org

With reverent gratitude, we heartily thank the contributing writers of this issue of Nectar of Nondual Truth, who have so graciously and selflessly shared the wisdom of their respective traditions and practices.

Staff of Nectar of Nondual Truth

Publisher
Sarada Ramakrishna Vivekananda Associations
* an Annual Publication

For more information concerning the SRV Associations or Nectar of Nondual Truth please contact:
SRV Associations, PO Box 1364, Honoka'a, HI 96727
Phone: (808) 990-3354
e-mail: srvinfo@srv.org   website: www.srv.org

Nectar Subscription is on a donation basis only
No part of this publication may be reproduced or transmitted in any form without permission from the publisher.
Entire contents copyright 2024. All Rights Reserved.
ISSN 1531-1414

Editor
Babaji Bob Kindler

Associate Editor
Annapurna Sarada

Production
Lokelani Kindler

Cover Image:
Photo by Amritatva Jack Jacobson

Acknowledgment
Image of Ramakrishna's Disciples
Courtesy of Vedanta Press
800-816-2242

Contributing Writers
Swami Brahmeshananda
Swami Sunirmalananda
Anam Thubten Rinpoche
Reverend Kosho Finch
Rabbi Rami Shapiro
Deacon Peter Solan
O.P. Sharma
Annapurna Sarada
Arurag Neal Aronowitz
Alexander Hixon
Babaji Bob Kindler

EDITORIAL

It is a great boon and a blessing to be able to offer to the contemporary world these teachings from the various religious traditions. Though not a very popular idea, or as yet a deeply accepted goal to attain among the earth's countries societies, and their peoples, it is nevertheless hoped that the proposal of the harmony of all religions will at least gain favor in those who desire to see the world become a better place, whether or not religion plays a prominent role in their daily lives.

And this is the reason why Nectar of Nondual Truth *cannot really present a cover to cover offering of pure nondualism, for besides being nearly impossible to actually express the essence of advaita/nonduality in words and writing, the fact remains that, if beings do indeed take to religion at all in these violent and intolerant times, they are still centering upon and gathering around thoughts and beliefs which speak in terms of God/Brahman being an entity separate from them. This settled conviction of the path of duality does not always allow for open concourse with the closeness or intimacy between creature and Creator, what to speak of the ready recognition of nonseparation between the apparent two.*

Therefore, the precious pieces of literary composition that infill this journal all fall in a wide spectrum between the poles of dualism and nondualism, with qualified nondualism (visishtadvaita) providing for their main basis and support. And for some unexplained and unintended reason, the subject of suffering has emerged in this issue, to be contemplated with a mind to reduce its influence and effects on humanity at large. It will never disappear from such a world as this, but lessening its scope and access — mainly to the human mind — would be a very fine penultimate goal to reach for.

On the completely opposite side of the picture, also represented in this issue of Nectar, is the rare but undeniable presence of Bliss, or Ananda, as termed by the Indian Rishis of old. It is suggested here on earth by the quality of happiness that is being pursued by all embodied beings, only itself being a much intensified version and also a lasting principle rather than a mere passing quality. This Bliss is based upon that ignorance-destroying Wisdom that facilitates its ongoing existence, whereas mere happiness is still heavily at risk from the fear of not-knowing and the phenomena of constant changefulness. Therefore, may all beings cause doubt to doubt itself, make fear afraid of itself, and place death in its own grave. As for changefulness, would that the permanence cited in all of Mother India's dharmas and darshanas make itself known to the human mind.

And speaking of change, the weather can be cited here, even in a philosophical journal. The world's exposure to Mother Nature's moods has been even more evident than usual of late. Further, the political climate has caught people's greater attention, as more and more of those noble and once-valued qualities in mankind such as honesty, cooperation, good will towards one's fellow man, and even common sense go missing. Thus, an article on what might be called religious and philosophical politics appears in this issue of Nectar of Nondual Truth, revealing how another ancient race, not only India, handled the human tendency to seek power in an overly insensitive manner and use it for selfish purposes rather than for the highest good of all.

These ideas, now buried a bit deep in collective consciousness, are the very ones which need rediscovery and resurrection. For, if the human being is divine by nature, as Swami Vivekananda reminded us of upon his arrival on the Western scene in 1893, and as Advaita Vedanta (nonduality) confirms in its wisdom scriptures through the pure minds and truthful lips of illumined seers such as he, then the remastery of the world and its powers should be a relatively simple matter. This is not an instance of a "power to the people" type of slogan followed by more violent actions, but rather a call to awaken to the divine Power (Shakti) already abiding in the people, followed by the effort to realize It.

Om Peace, Peace, Peace

Babaji Bob Kindler

NECTAR OF ADVAITIC INSTRUCTION

Questions from Our Readers

One great and seldomly shared secret of having Advaita as one's base for further spiritual comprehension, is that due to hearing it's one of a kind message, the inherent perfection of the Soul is already accepted prior to practice. Healing, growth, goal-orientation, and other modes of forward progress then prove to be subservient, at best.

"On certain days I am experiencing doubts as far as the spiritual and general life direction that I would like to take since initiation. It feels like I can't quite find a place where I feel empowered as a woman, whether along the path of Hinduism, or in the workplace in a male dominated profession. Is this just in me?"

Part of what Vedanta terms "the unreal" concerns gender. Not satisfied with the two primary genders that came to us naturally in life, people want to expand and have more genders. Thus there is contention. But Vedanta wants realization of what transcends all dualities, including genders. So people hold an immature definition of the word "transgender" nowadays. "Trans" means to transcend. The Atman has no gender. The real you is That. In it there exists true Oneness, not assumed or mistaken twoness; certainly not a third of fourth gender. All that is maya. Monasticism is the proof and example of this. When one calls oneself a man or a woman, one is misidentifying. We are neither body nor sex. Neither are we an American or a Hindu, an Easterner or a Westerner, etc. This is what Swami Vivekananda told his main female disciple, Sister Nivedita. You should read her books. A few are there on our SRV library shelves. You can also strike up a communication with sangha members on the subject.

Of course, in the conventional world, called the "straight" world by some, there are people who are misidentifying all the time. In Vedanta this is called thinking oneself to be the small self (ego) rather than knowing oneself to be the Great Self (Atman). If you set your divine feet upon the spiritual path, say of paths like Vedanta or Buddhism, you will simultaneously rid yourself of all false superimpositions (dualities) and embrace the Truth of your Eternal Being. Doing this leaves all contention behind forever, and results in Peace (shanti), and Bliss (ananda).

"Today's satsang and godblogs were beautifully insightful and keep stoking the reminder of vigilance in my discrimination and forbearance of the gunas. I also had a question that was answered in part during our discussion in the godblogs today regarding meditation, samskaras, and the scars that runs deeper than others. As one builds their fire of yoga through meditation practice, study of the scriptures, taking teachings with the guru, and asking questions, is there a more beneficial way to proceed with meditation concerning certain samskaras? Is it better to meditate on one's deep samskaras if they are recognized, and witness them first, or tackle of samskaras that may not run as deep? The thought in my mind is to build one's fire of yoga hot first and then proceed to meditate and burn away the deep scars (samskaras). However, there is the question of would it be more beneficial to focus on dissolving deep samskaras first, and in doing so one might easily dissolve more superficial samskaras later?"

Yes, and keeping in mind the phantom-like nature and substance of mental impressions, there is a way of popping that one main bubble of a samskara, which will then simultaneously pop the medium-sized and smaller bubbles that attach to it, as in a samskara-skandha. The usual way of going about this type of deep scrutiny and subconscious work is to take what is noticeably problematic and unwanted, and do away with that first. It is a more gradual way of going about it, and not as thorough, but most beings cannot drum up the force necessary to destroy the main impression at the source. This is all at the outset of practice. As practice deepens, then it becomes possible to dissolve impressions that are then obviously not in full alignment with the Truth of one's Being; so this is the medium grade way of proceeding, utilizing that very patience that we spoke about today at Satsang.

"How can we know, like in a close to death experience, if our time has come to leave the body or not?"

A "near death" experience passes so quickly that beings do not have the time to consider whether they are actually dying or not. They usually just go on living. And so it becomes a rather moot point. The teaching, then, is for action now, not to wait until any manner of calamity heads one's way, and death delivers its fatal blow totally unexpectedly. The more aware soul will come to know of its forthcoming passing if it remains near to God, to the Divine Mother who protects all life, and can prepare accordingly. Those who are far away from God never consider even the possibility, and are nearly always caught off guard. As our blessed Holy Mother, Sarada Devi, has said, *"Death keeps no office hours. Therefore, one must accomplish all necessary spiritual disciplines when young, if possible."*

"Could you please tell me your view on the perspective of the need to commit to one path only, and how then to integrate all that I have experienced and learned while attempting to choose one path? And do you feel that this teaching is right for me at this point? I do feel a strong heart resonance when I see and hear and feel all that SRV presents. It activates seeing in me and activates my love for Brahman as well. And it is also new to me to encounter an Advaita teacher who has so much attention for the concepts of the teachings, which I do appreciate a lot. And at the same time I also wonder if so much attention for the theory would not allow my mind to just create another phase of ego-identification around it."

To answer in proper order, the teachings we present are not "concept," nor are they "theory." They are Atmajnan, eternal verities of the revealed scriptures. One does not read them like books, but hears them as transmission from the revered preceptor of a timeless lineage and puts them into practice. This gets clarified for students early on if they discriminate arightly and take up one path and one teacher at the outset of spiritual life.

So that is my "view," but is also the traditional view of India and her illumined souls, gurus, and acharyas. Noncomprehension of this fundamental perspective (plus the lack of understanding of the nature of nonduality) is responsible for so much of the misdirection and falling off of the path by novitiate Western aspirants. In short, they do not understand the path of Guru Yoga. It is not just the cause of the selecting of too many paths, gurus, and mantras problem that we see all the time now, but the inability to have full confidence in one's powers of discrimination and thus remain devoted to the selected ideal one's entire life.

For, and to shine an even clearer light upon this matter, beings who embody to, as Sri Krishna states in the Gita, *"continue on with the thread of their Yogic path,"* do not find themselves in a mode of hopeful search for a teacher when they arrive on earth again, but rather are in the process of remembering the guru they had in their previous lifetime(s). For them, it becomes a matter of "tracking the scent," as it were, like a bloodhound would. Others, transgressing the laws and tenets of Guru Yoga, often unknowingly, cast about, randomly, and try to find a teacher based upon the unreliable winds of past karmas combined with their own egoic emotions and sentimental feelings. One will see them, bouncing like silver balls inside of a pinball machine, from one path to another, one instructor to another, often wondering why they cannot settle down. Some devotion may mount up; but where to store it? Some jnanam may accumulate, but who to invest it in? Some yogic power may store up, even, but it also risks falling into attraction for the power in nature and the occult power in the human psyche.

So, just like, in any form of yoga, the senses need to be controlled at the outset, and the mind's restlessness requires calming, the heart's fickleness and tendency to betray its original, God-given direction, has to be quelled. A start along the pathway of authentic Guru Yoga will kick in, and will probably surface as divine memory in the transmigrating soul's succeeding lifetime — as is the case with so many others. As the Upanisads state, *"Godspeed to you in crossing over to the farthest shore beyond all darkness."*

"You said something about the Goddess Tripurasundari, that Her mantra could be divided into three parts that would, with time and patience, reveal themselves to the practitioner. Could you elaborate on that for me please, just lightly? Otherwise, the mantra practice is going well. I understand that patience and time are really vital regarding that, as you have told me so many times. It's a subtle practice which embodies and symbolizes the humble and sweet aspects of spiritual life."

Yes, the triple aspect of Tripura Sundari is the deity associated with the sacred words of the mantra. She is the intelligence in the utterances, in all mantras. The mantra I gave you was the first part of the holy three, the audible sound of it and its power for transformation. When you concentrate deep within with the mantra, and over time, Her second aspect will come forth and reveal itself. Give that some years and some practice, as you refer to here. At the end of mantra practice the third aspect will become revealed, offering the final fruits of the practice. All of purification on its many levels will have become completed by then. In the meantime give all that you have into the meditation surrounding the mantra and the Devi.

"The Bhagavad Gita Jayanti is coming up on the 22nd of December. I would like to finish committing to memory the 2nd chapter by then. I am at the 61st verse. What are some strong, positive Samskaras that can be adopted to help remain in Sthiti Prajnasya? In the second chapter of the Bhagavad Gita Krishna talks mostly of how Arjuna should remain unaffected by the impending war and become even minded. But there should be certain methods to adopt. I understand that even in a solitary atmosphere the mind can become turbulent, Pramathini as stated in the 60th verse. Shri Krishna says that to attain steady wisdom one should think of him, but what does that imply?

Once real wisdom is digested, over a period of time, in company of the guru and consultation with the scriptures, steady wisdom, sthiti prajnasya will verily settle in naturally. One will hardly even notice the going away of ignorance held over lifetimes, as it dies in stages. As Ramprasad sings, *"I can no longer practice formal meditation at the sacred times of dawn and dusk, because the sun of Her wisdom never rises nor sets."* And this "return" to inherent wisdom is one's own, natural state, only carelessly abandoned earlier due to unwise thoughts and inadvertent acts. The nectar of naturalness has returned, then, and one needs only live in it, and pass it on to others, until the body drops away like a blown off leaf in a gale.

"I would like to comment about the most recent god blog that you posted to say that I think this perspective of having our ancestors as monkeys has caused a lot of mischief in the minds of the masses, including myself at times, because we think it is okay to act and think as animals. But it is so important to make a distinction. There can be such a perspective as to think that we have evolved from being animals and how now, we think rationally, but it is still a very primitive way of thinking. Such scientific nihilism x's out many ways of expanding our consciousness, as the sages of India have done."

This scientific perspective is based upon being unaware of the human soul, and its direct connection to God as Consciousness. Until Consciousness is brought into the picture, no higher view will intervene on our behalf. We will be assigned the comparatively ignoble station of an animal, as unthinkable as that is...

"What is the difference between Vedanta and Hinduism? Is there a difference? I have heard that there is, but I don't understand enough to know."

As for Hinduism, it is conventional Indian religion. Just as there is real Christianity existing in places, there is also conventional Christianity present as well. Hinduism is like this too. But in India there is known to be Vedanta, based in Upanisads rather than in dualistic religion. Vedanta transcends mundane human convention and fundamentalist religion. It also has a higher leaning called Advaita, or Nonduality. SRV is teaching that, mainly, but it leaves room for people to approach it in their own time (but without too much delay, thus risking forgetfulness).

"I was wanting to ask you what chants you use when you are called to attend the passing of a living being. Our family dog passed away this Saturday, who has been with us since 2010, and my father had asked me to say some appropriate prayers for her. I had chanted the Purnamadah prayer, the Dhyahu shantih prayer, and the Asato maa sat gamah prayer, successively. Are these effective prayers for the passing of a soul, or would you recommend something else?"

Pertaining to departed beings, for an animal, what you did, like an overall peace chant, was good. For a human being, who has deeper consciousness, a more personal prayer can be offered. Even then, these offerings are as much or more for those left behind as for the departed, who are already in another place, so to speak.

"Throughout the many years of my spiritual practice, I have used different intoxicants to induce deeper moods. Though I feel that it benefitted me, of late I feel like it is beginning to limit me, and I think that the phase may be coming to an end. The ups and downs that these substances caused while I was under their influence also bothers me. What would you advise?"

Taking an intoxicant simultaneously creates a samskara for taking the intoxicant in the mind. It also creates a karma for ingesting it. That is why there are negative effects which come back on people. Sincere and pure spiritual austerities do not throw back negativities on the practitioner, but rather open the path deeper, free of those ups and downs the likes of what you have experienced along the way. Further, adding in an intoxicant to one's spiritual practice weakens one's will. It undermines one's inherent power to realize perfection and attain it on one's own merit, rather than by other means. My advice and even my prayer, is: may people stand on their own two legs, ingest pure food, breathe pure air, contemplate pure teachings, worship pure luminaries, and swiftly reach the Goal of human existence free of all unnecessary weights and impediments. God knows that there are plenty obstacles heading our way already.....

"When Sri Krishna says, in the 11th verse of the second chapter of the Gita, that the wise don't grieve for the dead nor the living, how should I understand this properly?"

Because the true Self is never born and never dies, the wise do not grieve. The coming and passing of the body is grieved only by those who think the body is the soul, or do not know of the existence of the soul at all. They might feel the loss of a loved one, but that is the presence of Atman in the body (not the body itself) that they miss. Thus, and similarly, "It is not for the sake of the baby that the baby is loved, but for the sake of the Atman in the baby"...as Yajnavalkya states.....

"During the day impure thoughts come up many times. I am wondering what an 'impure thought' is considered in our lineage. I have assumptions/inferences, but wanted to ask you about that. There are so many thoughts of desire that enter my day and it's hard in this culture to imagine even a series of moments where I wouldn't have them, even the desire to improve my social capacity, to make others comfortable, to be around like-minded people, they're all desires, or seem to be."

As we agreed prior to your initiation, your practice must be peppered with attendance at SRV events, as much as possible. You know some of the people quite well, so be with your family as often as you can. Such presence will help impure thoughts diminish. Sri Ramakrishna said, that in this particular age and time, impure thoughts cannot harm one unless they are acted upon. So try to turn towards healthy thoughts when these others rise up, and do not act upon their suggestion. Otherwise, that is how karmas get formed and return upon us. Raise an opposite wave, as you may have heard.

Desires, overall, can be quite natural – like to have food, to fulfill oneself, etc. One needs only discriminate between those desires that tend to bind one in attachment, and those desires which lead to, and end in, fulfillment. There is a good chart in the "Footfalls of the Indian Rishis" book on that, from Holy Mother.

"Is the ocean in the wave or is the wave in the ocean? The wave is obviously in the ocean since it collapses and dissolves back into it. The ocean is Brahman and the wave is...? The seeker can think of themself as the water. I would like to understand what/who the wave is in the metaphor, and why the seekers can think of themselves as water. The waves make me think of vrittis, but in this case I don't think they represent that."

The wave in this metaphor/analogy, represents the individual human ego, or the soul if one wants to use it that way. The ocean, Brahman, emits souls, as it were, like an ocean forms waves The forms are transitory, fleeting, and many. The ocean is ever-one. Water is the all-pervasive substance that exists equally and undivided in and through all these ego-soul waves, and which is their essence. It represents the Atman. If the ego identifies with its wave form (made partly of vrittis), it suffers birth and death, coming and going, etc., but if it can identify with the essence, called water, then it can merge itself with the ocean. At that time it will only associate with waves/forms when they appear, from then on.

"During the class you were talking about how Ishwara is considered to be the highest form, and in connection with the Holy Trio. You were also saying that Ishwara is still inferior to formlessness. But one still needs to reach the stage of being aware of Ishwara, I believe. I have been practicing being the witness of my mind during meditation. I sometimes see how my mind wanders from time to time; but just by keeping some witness of these thoughts my mind naturally comes back into focus. A lot of the classes that we have been hearing from you lately talk about principles. I would like to be more aware of the tattwas, and would like to somehow reach a higher platform of understanding through tapasya. My question is, should the grossest form of the tattwas, the Pancha Mahabhutas, be considered as existing within the mind while meditating on them? I was always trying to imagine them external, but I find that there is an essence of them within the mind, and how they make up the physical form."

Trust that I did not use the word "inferior" with regards to Ishvara. Speaking in terms of form and formlessness, this may be the case, when Brahman is realized, for every form springs from mind, and gets put together in some way. Islands are forms, but they appear in formless oceans. Clouds are forms, and they come forth from open skies. Ice cubes are forms, and they solidify from liquid waters. Avatars by the numbers are forms, but come to us through the Trinity who spring from the Ocean of formless Awareness, where even Vishnu sleeps at the time of Mahapralaya.

About the Pancha Mahabhutas, in life we observe them at first as outer elements in their external manifestation. This is prior to even our five senses becoming fully developed. The very fact that things grow, develop, and mature is a sign that such principles are incomplete in their external manifestations. It is why they cannot fulfill or satisfy us as well. To know the five elements closer to the source, which is why Patanjali wants meditation upon them, is to discover the tanmatras. Both elements and senses can and should be traced to them. Lack of this verification is the cause for people not having an inner life, as Jesus told. Science has no inner life, being unaware of the tanmatras. An individual, a culture, needs a well-developed philosophy in order to get teachings and perceive principles such as they. Prana, too, has gone unnoticed in most of the world, even since before the birth of Jesus.

Mind, beyond brain and ordinary thought vibrations, holds the secrets and origins to all the tattvas. By meditating upon them as alambanas, it can pierce through the abiding superstitions of religion and science. When this is accomplished, then we can speak about such glorious Truths as the Atman.

"Thank you for the Satsang today. I was happy to be able to attend and hear everyone's questions and your responses to them which was compounded by me not making classes recently and travelling. Doubt is on my mind in regards to many elements of my existence here on the planet. I find myself doubting my ability to travel down a spiritual path that is all-accepting and truly all-loving and pervasive as I sense there is ancestral guilt that likely comes from having a very hard-line of parenting stemming from a Baptist upbringing. Visiting family always has me reflecting on this. I see and feel theirgood hearts but I hear traces of judgment and feel anger emanating from them, which also echoes in my own mind. We often discuss many issues related to the body, as they are aging quite a lot. There was so much fear and panic there, and I completely get it. It has me thinking about deeper questions such as the attachment I have to my own body, health, and well-being. Of course these things are important, but how can we disengage to where it doesn't create such immense suffering when something changes in our lives and in our bodies? Also, how do we effectively disengage from our ancestors, or heal and work with our ancestors? How can I transcend this panic and fear that I also feel that I see in my family while visiting with them? Furthermore, how can I disengage from the body to the point that I wouldn't feel such deep pain and suffering."

Your fresh presence among the sangha is timely, seeing that you are coming up against the challenges of embodiment in this world. We have to give the body its due, though without catering to it alone, as so many people fall victim to doing. It is very fortunate that we are not the body, as Vedanta reminds us, and it seems we have to take this teaching over and over again until it sticks in the mind. When it does, one gets released into a finer level of consciousness based in transcendent thought, or higher/deeper thought. That is what you heard today, and also why everyone joins Satsang weekly in order to run the teachings deep into the mind's thinking process (samskaras). When we see our family, we actually visit our ancestors, as family usually translates as beings whom one incarnated with in earlier lifetimes. As such, seeing them reminds us of our predicament in maya, or, if we have divine ancestry, as many in India have, then we get reminded of our divine heritage. At present you have both, like on two sides, and the divine side is trying to awaken you to your true nature, Atman, via initiation, guru, sangha, and teachings.

Few beings, like your father and grandfather, ever received these special transmissions, so you are fortunate. You can also, by realizing them, pass them on to your earth family by becoming grounded in them, thus freed. The teachings say that an enlightened soul can free 7 generations of his or her birth family in both directions, past and future. This is how important spiritual life and its aims are in the process of embodiment.

As far as your own suffering goes, take it as a lesson rather than a misfortune, as a test rather than a trouble, as a boon rather than a curse. Through such trials the wise one develops detachment from the body, while the unwise only develop fear and aversion. Now and after, let the thought of disease roll off of you like water off of a duck's feathers. Therefore you will not take it with you into later life, or into future births. For, if the soul imagines that suffering is real instead of only a passing phenomenon, then it will lend it strength instead of seeing it only as a matter of the moment. This is the way to overcome diseases.

"I love what I have learned reading certain books at SRV like Jnana Yoga, the Gita, and parts of your books, and what I've taken from the classes taught by you. Regardless, it feels like I can't quite get my base beneath me. Will voicing these doubts help, along with connecting to spiritual community."

The soul must learn to discipline itself in order to reach continual peace of mind. Guru and sangha are helpmates towards that necessary discipline. It is interesting that you once told me that work, obligations, and doubts and fears "wipe away" the benefits of the Saturday satsang. It should be the other way, i.e., that attending upon Satsang, hearing the truth, and keeping company with the devotees, will wipe all of those lesser considerations away, helping one start anew the following day/week. Since nothing is important except Reality, all that is not reality, that is relativity, can be sacrificed, and this act is to be done every week. That is one's best possession in life; it is called renunciation.

By thoughts of Reality alone, neutralize all that is changing and unstable. First it is called detachment. Then it becomes outright renunciation. Ironically, neither would be necessary if attachment to the world had not been in the mind at birth. So, either renounce the unreal (changing), or love the Real (Unchanging).

The former negates the nonessential; the latter embraces the Essential/Essence. These are the two primary paths. And they can be combined if one wants freedom sooner than later.

"I heard you say that if we can get control of the psychic prana, then the gross prana will naturally come under our control as well. I just want to check my understanding on that. What I'm thinking, is because all manifest phenomenon is a projection from the mind, it would make sense that if one has control of the mind and all thoughts, that it would lead to a complete control of one's external existence as well. But I'm assuming that, because of the state of the world today, there will always be some chance of being in situations that are out of our control, and what we do have control of is how we react or not react to things. I also liked hearing you say that by the physical practice of stilling the body in meditation, we are shown that we must also have an ability to completely still the mind."

Controlling the prana is a necessary penultimate step to controlling the mind, i.e., psychic prana. So yes, successful detachment and discrimination, along with the levels of meditation, are all dependent on that. Spontaneous action is also possible along the way. Do keep studying the Raja Yoga lessons to fill in all gaps in understanding.

"At the darkest time of the year I would like to wish you an insightful Dipawali and Kali puja. We just finished the Lakshmi Kubera Puja together. I always try to aim for an earlier time to write and I am not satisfied that I could not write to you before. I have been watching this week's class on Sadhakya and the cosmic principles. The teaching of everything coming from the mind has really hit me on this occasion, and I saw this teaching in a different perspective than usual. We should always look at our life in a way so as to recognize everything as mind. Because we operate from our mind, and all of our activities are dependent on it, we might as well consider everything external as being the mind. My meditations have been going well. Everyone's sharing at the fellowship meeting recently was very powerful. Some of it entailed a host of guided meditations that you wrote in the book of Durga's 10 divine articles. I would like to get more and more immersed in the thoughts of Sri Ramakrishna, Holy Mother, and Swami Vivekananda, and always operate from this awareness and their blessings."

Yes, the radiant blackness. It is seen in stark contrast to the light of the physical sun and etheric lights of heaven to those who go deeper in their meditation on Consciousness. And such depths occur to the individual when realizations such as everything being an expression of the mind dawns. It is not just a saying, or a good teaching, but is more that, literally, all solid objects are thought concretized. Belief in the idea that all things have an outer origin (science/physics), in and of themselves, has thwarted the mind from knowing the outside to be mental projection. One becomes a slave of time and crippled occupier of space by such a belief.

"Before I took on the body, there was nothing to realize because I 'was' Atman. Nothing was that didn't belong to me. I had everything as I was everything; Nature included. Yet I fell. You have always taught me that I am Atman. Now I'm more confused. I'll die like this. It will take lifetimes to realize Atman now – that is, if there are in fact lifetimes after this. I will attempt to continue my practice. I will continue to read what I can. I struggle to read lengthy material; I can't get through a book. This is why I call it Kindergarten level when I say I need it explained on a child's reading level. Like, I am not convinced that there's a life after this anymore. I am no longer convinced that I was once or am Atman, so pure and complete. Especially now considering that nature is more powerful than Atman, since it took Atman into a body. I'm not questioning suffering. I am aware of where that's coming from. I'm questioning the next thing. In fact I am almost no longer questioning. I used to be convinced that there was something after. I was convinced that there is Mother, God, Brahman. Right now I'm not convinced, and falling into being convinced that there is nothing, like deeper into atheism."

Renounce both what is appearing now in front of you, and what supposedly comes after. And as a Vedantist, Buddhist, and lover of God/guru, you must accomplish that renunciation on the truth of "Everything Is," and "I Am." Since you know this in your heart, it is only your mind's confusion that thwarts you. Why let confusion win over your higher and hard-won spiritual view? You might as well let the devil of your past take the guru of your present away; will you allow that? That confusion you complain of will disappear tomorrow, or the next day. Then you will be fine for a time. It is all the play of the gunas/thoughts in the mind. You are presently doing the practice of remaining steady. What does that have to do with an afterlife, or a post-mortem emancipation? That is all conjecture, all imagination. It is all a test for your as yet unmastered mind. Find your favorite position, your preferred mental asana, and hold it, like you would hold a long breath in order to see how fit your lungs are. Reserve your conclusions around believer, atheist, etc., until you have controlled the mind. Pure mind will give you the best view of Truth; certainly will not give you a confused mind. Patience and perseverance are real enough, yes? Just never give up.

"Your response was written in a manner I understood. Thank you. However, I'm still confused. I guess the question then is, I am the Atman so why would I, as Atman, dare take on a body and want possessions or outside stimuli, when I have everything. When I AM everything. How did we fall weak from Atman?"

For, a simple answer to the Atman query is that we do not know It fully, particularly here, in the embodied condition. As the Great Master said it, simply, "When one finally tastes boiled, refined sugar candy, one will give up eating treacle right away." When we come to know our Self, then, we will abandon these competing forms lurking in nature. To put it in Swamiji's words, "When one attains a higher vision, one will let go of the lower vision naturally." As Lord Buddha put it, "Suffering is." In other words, you cannot have pure pleasure and happiness in nature due to the pain inherent in birth, growth, disease, old age, decay, and death. These are all happily missing in your Buddha Nature (Atman). Body and ego go together. If one takes on one, the other comes along for the ride. In between them is mind, holding nature in it, with all of nature's allurements. When the disembodied soul sees that mechanism (mind/ego/body) and sees its powers (nature), it jumps in, inadvisably. When it identifies with all of that (the unreal), it forgets the Atman (the only Reality).

"Apart from the godblogs and the Sunday class that I have been listening to, I would like to ask about how the Atman never moves. This is a big question for me, that has only recently been more perceptible for me, and your teachings on it brings some clarity to the subject. Swami Abedananda writes: 'Take a cup, or a bottle, or an empty bottle, and move it from here to the street, or take it from here to a distant place. Now, you know the bottle, or the cup, or the jar, is moving, and it is true that it is moving, but think of the space that is in the bottle. Is the space, confined in the jar, moving? When you move this jar from one place to another, the space appears to be moving with the jar. But does it move really? No, the space never moves. What does move then? It is the jar that moves. But can the jar exist outside of space? No it does not. Yet we say that it is moving. The very extension of the body means limitation in space. You are moving the body from one part of space to another part. But does it really move? The space does not move. So the movement of the space is relative and apparent to the senses. But our senses are so deceptive and our mind is so limited and our intellect is so imperfect, we think that we are moving constantly. Again, the central substance appears to move, yet it does not move. It appears to be born, yet it is unborn.'"

Yes, the metaphor of the bottle in your selected excerpt is an adequate one for demonstrating the immovability of the Atman, or Conscious Awareness — It being so subtle, that it is not displaceable. One could cite the air in the bottle as being transferable from place to place, so we could call the air our thinking minds identifying with the body, which would be the bottle. As the bottle and air got exposed to different colors outside, they would take on the attributes of various things, which would be our thoughts.

An advaitic analogy for all this would be how the physical body does not move when the dream body goes from locale to locale (like Gaudapada's famous analogy of the runner running a race in a dream while sleeping, in the Karika on the Mandukya Upanisad). Since we are identified with the dream body at night, our involved witness observes changes in location, and this also happens when we leave the body on earth and ascend inwardly to the heavenly spheres of existence. We are shifting lokas in this case, but only from the standpoint of the transmigrating soul (mind), not from the perspective of boundary-less Consciousness. The latter exists free of bodies, and as the body moves due to prana, and the thought body moves by means of psychic prana, You, as Awareness, if you have realized It, remain the stationary Overseer. This is why we say that Consciousness is all-pervasive, and being everywhere in time and space, as well as beyond time and space, sees and knows all and everything simultaneously, i.e., the 3 Om's (Omniscience, Omnipresence, Omnipotence).

This is why we hear that earth (humankind), heaven (ancestors), and Vaikuntha (gods and Ishvara) are essentially nondifferent; they all exist in immovable Consciousness, i.e., in You. Slough off the body filter and you see the ancestors; remove the dual mind filter and you see the celestials, then gods, and then God — all standing permanently in one Divine Place...the Locus of Illimitable Love.

"Why would God lodge in a body to suffer its way back to itself?"

As I have repeated many times, Brahman, God, does nothing. It is actionless; It is karmaless. So please accept this bit of important clarification and never blame the Eternally Perfect for all of mind's imperfections again. With Mother, She also does not want us to suffer, but in Her case, She watches over Her children. Those children, themselves, want to do this thing or that thing (possess and enjoy), and go to this place and that place has (heaven, earth, and hell). She will not necessarily advise it, and even often advises against it; but they will not listen to Her. No, my dear: We must blame no one but ourselves for our suffering; also, for taking on bodies and desiring the things and objects of this earth realm. Give it all up here, on earth, with its lesson of "suffering is," and you will not have to return here again. Nor will you go to heaven, where more insipid pleasures await, for you will have transcended the desire for realms of selfish activity altogether. As Holy Mother told us, "That will be your last lifetime when you git rid of desires." In the meantime, you can fulfill them in the dharma.....

When we first began this journey, you and I, I gave you the Sri Sarada Vijnanagita to read, bedside style. Now you can take up its companion, the Swami Vivekananda Vijnanagita. For questions the like of which you write to me here can be very well answered with that book. Sorry if this message is not on the level of a child, as you asked, but the truth is that you are not one anymore, neither in age, nor in spiritual understanding. Move on, in, up...and stop not til the goal is reached.

"Between 'the mind' and 'the Mind,' which is greater?"

First, both body and mind follow the Will. Since will is a property of the mind, the mind is superior. Next, in the case of worldly persons (egos), the body proves itself the master, whereas for beings who live in the mind's intelligence and higher awareness, the mind overshadows body and senses, both. The strength of the body and senses cannot be denied for they can even influence intellectuals and others who champion mind over matter. Third, ordinary mind may as well be the body. For most beings, that is called the brain, and is located in the body. Higher Mind is Atman. So, when one says "I am not the mind," they are making a shift beyond thought and transcendent of the intellectual frame of reference — both of these used by the ego daily. In the case of beings overworking the body, brain is acting as the body, with no real discrimination of its own, like in the animals. This is why the sensitive being after spirituality sits and stills the body with one asana, then slows the breathing to arrest it, and finally dissolves the thoughts back into the intellect. Body and brain (and ego) are then made to bow to higher Awareness. To perceive higher Awareness, however, one needs to practice identifying with It daily, since consciousness tends to return to the mind's ordinary thought, the ego's misguided and often arrogant dictates, the senses pleasures (and pains), and the body's functions.

Questions regarding problems in spiritual life may be directed to Nectar's editorial staff at: srvinfo@srv.org

◆ *Swami Brahmeshananda*

THE ANATOMY OF SUFFERING
The Eloquent Language of Pain

The ancient sage, Narada, approached another great saint, Sanat Kumar, for instruction. Sanat Kumar asked what Narada already knew, so that he might instruct accordingly. Narada gave a long list of subjects he had mastered: the Vedas, their subsidiaries, history, mythology, and various sciences and humanities, and confessed that in spite of all this knowledge, he had still not gone beyond sorrow.

That was in ancient times. But even now people suffer, the learned probably more than the ignorant. The only difference is that they don't seek the advice of saints and sages but consult psychiatrists. And they do not say that they are suffering. Instead they say that they have anxiety or depression, phobia or insomnia. There are others who do not even go to the psychiatrist. They try alcohol, tranquilizers or antidepressants. Some do not even recognize the symptoms of mental agony and don't consult a psychiatrist or a physician. As a result they land up either in a mental asylum or a prison. But then, they are not saints like Narada and their misfortune is understandable. But why should sages like Narada suffer?

The fact is that every one suffers. Suffering is a universal phenomenon that none escape. The saint and the sinner, the rich and the poor, the learned and the ignorant, the old and the young, all suffer in some form or another. And all have been eternally trying to get rid of suffering and to obtain lasting happiness. The ironic thing, however, is that in spite of all these attempts for ages and ages, suffering has persisted. It may not have increased, but it has not decreased by any means. Let us therefore study what, after all, is this thing called suffering, so that, knowing its nature, we may go beyond it.

Grades and Types of Suffering

One way of classifying suffering is according to the causative agency. Suffering can be caused by natural calamities like floods, droughts, cyclones, etc. Or it can be caused by other creatures: flies, mosquitoes, snakes, scorpions, beasts, other human beings, etc. Finally suffering can be of our own making. The latter can be physical or mental. These three types of sufferings are called *tritàpa*. While one may ward off suffering due to other creatures and take precautions against natural calamities, the sufferings of which we ourselves are responsible are the ones which are really within our reach, and we can do something worthwhile to get over them.

There can be various grades of severity of suffering, from bearable head-aches and body-aches to the unbearable pain of cancer. Mental suffering can also range from a mild, bearable degree of just an uncomfortable feeling, to an intense and unbearable degree capable of causing mental breakdown. The extreme calamity which befell the Buddhist nun Pakachara before she found peace at the feet of Lord Buddha, can be cited as an example of extreme mental suffering. On her way to her parent's home with her husband and a son, Pakachara gave birth to a child. Her husband went in search of water but did not return. He died of snake bite. Pakachara tried to cross the river with her two children. The new-born baby was snatched away by a vulture, and in an attempt to save it, the other boy was swept away in the running stream. And finally, on reaching the house of her parents, she found it burnt to ashes with no survivors. Who could forbear such calamities, following one after the other in such quick succession?

A Biological Analysis

A large part of human, and even animal, suffering is physical. In this context it may be mentioned that the less evolved a creature is, the greater is its physical suffering. As the organism evolves and becomes more and more complex, the mechanism of suffering too becomes more and more complex. This would become all the more clear if we trace the evolution of the mechanism of suffering from an amoeba to a fully evolved human being with a complex nervous system.

We don't know whether an amoeba has anything like suffering as we humans look at it. In it there is only attraction and repulsion, and its whole being responds to these processes. Indeed, it is only these processes of attraction and repulsion in response to something beneficial or harmful that evolve into likes and dislikes, and ultimately into pain and pleasure. The amoeba throws out pseudopodea to engulf a desired object or recoils from anything harmful. These reactions are essential for its survival and existence. In creatures with a rudimentary nervous system, this very process of attraction and repulsion assumes the form of a reflex action. A leech would reflexly recoil from a harmful chemical. The severed tail of a lizard would reflexly jump about for some time. The trunk of an animal whose head is severed would reflexly toss about, and so on. In all these cases, since there is no brain, there would not be "pain" in the sense we generally understand. The reaction to painful situations is ingrained, as it were, in the nervous system of these creatures.

With the evolution of the brain, happiness and misery, pleasure and pain, are distinctly felt and recorded. Instead of acting reflexly, creatures with a brain react instinctively. But, although these animals with a brain can feel and express pleasure and pain, they cannot differentiate between themselves and their pain or pleasure, and their instinctive reactions are basically similar to repulsion and attraction of an amoeba or reflex action of lower creatures. In all these creatures anything conducive to survival is considered "pleasant," while anything threatening it is considered "painful." Subhuman animals and creatures cannot think of past or future, and their experiences in life are stored in the form of instincts and reflex actions.

It would be evident from the fore-going that "pain" is a factor or characteristic which nature has ingrained into the physical body of an organism for its defense and survival. To this a nervous system has been added in animals, and a highly evolved brain in humans. Human beings alone have the ability to experience pain and pleasure as distinct and separate from themselves. Subhuman creatures, therefore, feel far more intense physical pain and pleasure. In fact, these feelings in them are not separate from their being. An understanding of this fact is extremely important for the transcendence of suffering.

In spite of having the ability to transcend suffering by not identifying with it, most human beings, and specially children, act instinctively like animals. Children, with fractured thigh or hip bones, are made to hang almost upside down with their legs tied upwards as a part of the treatment. Even in such an uncomfortable and unaccustomed position, they quickly adjust and play with toys. In an almost similar manner, a child, blind by birth, would adjust and learn to live with his four senses. So also a child with an inborn defect like a respiratory disease.

Psychological Analysis

With the development of cerebral hemispheres — the part of the brain responsible for intellect — what are called mental sufferings make their appearance. With the introduction of the faculty of emotions and intellect, humans no more respond to situations reflexly or instinctively like animals. Likes and dislikes, attachments and aversions, desires and ambitions, make their appearance. And these are the major causes of mental suffering. Encountering an unpleasant situation, person or object, *anishta yoga*, and parting with a desired situation, person or place, *ishta-viyoga*, cause sorrow.

Apart from needs for survival, for which intellect, like instincts, is geared, wants and desires not directly related to survival are also born. Let us take an example: A child, born and brought up in a poor village home, is used to sleeping on the floor, with a mat spread on it. It is used to a simple food and a hard life, and obviously, they do not appear painful to him. For, they satisfy his needs very well. Now, suppose this child were to come and live in a town in a room furnished with soft cushions, fans, and other comforts; he would, by comparison, feel that he had suffered privations so far in the village, and living under old conditions now would appear painful to him! Though his needs are the same, his artificial wants have changed.

Other causes of suffering are fear and anxiety. It is said that everything is fraught with fear: *"In enjoyment there is the fear of disease; in social position the fear of failure; in wealth, the fear of hostile kings; in honor, the fear of humiliation; in power the fear of enemies; in beauty, the fear of old age; in scriptural erudition, the fear of opponents; in virtue, the fear of traducers; in body the fear of death..."* Fear and anxiety are related to the future. Arjuna became miserable on the battle-field imagining the future consequences of the war. Others live in the past and continue to mourn their mistakes, or lament upon an expected pleasant event which did not come to pass. "Oh, had

> "In enjoyment there is the fear of disease; in social position the fear of failure; in wealth, the fear of hostile kings; in honor, the fear of humiliation; in power the fear of enemies; in beauty, the fear of old age; in scriptural erudition, the fear of opponents; in virtue, the fear of traducers; in body the fear of death..."

I not done this I would not have suffered like this." "Oh, I did not perform that meritorious act; also I committed those sins"; lamenting thus, people suffer. One old lady was traveling in a crowded railway compartment with her grown up son who, for want of space, was sleeping on the floor between two berths. Suddenly a heavy article fell from above, a hair's breadth away from the sleeping young man. Now, instead of being thankful to God and feeling happy that her son had been miraculously saved, the old lady went on mourning the rest of the journey about what would have happened had the load fallen on her son! We often live in our world of imagination, past or future, and suffer. Living in the future causes worry and anxiety, and living in the past causes depression, and these are the forms of suffering which have become most common in modern times. In a sense, animals are better off, since they live in the present and do not mourn their past nor plan for the future.

A sense of insecurity, basically related to the survival instinct, is another form of suffering, which is beautifully depicted in the story of "The lost child." It wanted toys, sweets, etc., to begin with. But the moment it found that it was lost and that its parents were no longer with it, it became disconsolate and the former objects of attraction did not interest it any longer.

With social, cultural, moral, and spiritual evolution of human beings and with the refinement of their tastes, the character of their suffering too changes. A person without musical sense might not feel the least discomfort on hearing a poorly sung, out-of-tune, song. But to a musician, the slightest disharmony would cause intense discomfort. Similarly, a moralist with a highly evolved ethical sense would feel deeply hurt by the moral lapses in people around, and more so in himself, which in a morally insensitive person might not cause any problem. An uncultured aborigine might not hesitate to kill another if it served his selfish interest. There might be another person on the other extreme of the moral scale, who might feel guilty even if an ill-feeling towards someone were to cross his mind. Wealth and possessions are positive means of joy

> "...even prophets have to suffer, and probably to a much greater degree. Ramachandra had to live for fourteen years in the forest. Sita's life was one of continuous suffering. Jesus, the Christ, was crucified. The yogis fare no better. For them everything is painful, even apparently pleasing objects and events. They, by their discrimination, are able to detect the crown of misery over the head of happiness."

for almost everyone. But for Sri Ramakrishna, money was a definite source of pain. A lover of freedom would gladly bear all sufferings for it, and would never like to forfeit his freedom at any cost.

What about spiritual aspirants, the *yogis*, and illumined souls? Are they not immune to suffering? After all, all their struggles and labors are to go beyond suffering and attain everlasting happiness. No, it is just the opposite. As we have seen in the case of Sri Ramakrishna, even prophets have to suffer, and probably to a much greater degree. Ramachandra had to live for fourteen years in the forest. Sita's life was one of continuous suffering. Jesus, the Christ, was crucified. The *yogis* fare no better. For them everything is painful, even apparently pleasing objects and events. They, by their discrimination, are able to detect the crown of misery over the head of happiness. Most enjoyments consequently produce pain. Then there is the fear of loss, since nothing in the world is lasting. Besides, fresh cravings arise from impressions of happiness. And finally, due to the clash between different forces of nature, one dragging in one direction and another in another, permanent happiness becomes impossible.

To summarize, pain and suffering are inseparably connected with existence. In subhuman creatures with strong identification with the body, and in less cultured human beings with equally strong body-consciousness, suffering is mainly physical, and is mostly related to the survival instinct. In the more evolved individuals, mental suffering predominates and is proportional to the intensity of the individual's likes and dislikes, ambitions, desires and aspirations, ideals and principles. In animals, pain is an indicator of disharmony and a factor directing, helping, and encouraging evolution. In humans, the type of suffering indicates the cultural evolution of an individual and shows his points of psychological vulnerability. For, misery is mostly of our own making. Pain is the most eloquent language of the unhealthy body or mind. It comes to convey an important message. Instead of being afraid of it, let us learn to read the message.

A former editor of the Vedanta Keshari, and previously of the Ramakrishna Mission Home of Service, Swami Brameshananda is a senior monk of the Ramakrishna Order and until recently was the Secretary of the Ramakrishna Mission Ashram in Chandigarh, India. Over the years his writings in Hindi and English have appeared in several journals, including Prabuddha Bharata, Vedanta Keshari, and Nectar of Nondual Truth. He specializes in themes related to Jainism. He is now retired and is living an inner, contemplative life in Varanasi.

Select Verses of Bhartrihari

Going searching in the lower regions,
going into the skies,
Traveling through all the worlds,
this is but the fickleness of the mind.
Ah, friend, you never remember the Lord Who
resides within you.
How can you get happiness!

What is there in the reading of Vedas,
The Shrutis, the Purânas, doing sacrifices?
Freedom alone takes off the weight
of this dreadful world,
And manifests Self-blessedness.
Here is the truth: the rest is all shop-keeping.

When the body is still healthy, diseaseless,
When old age has not yet attacked it,
When the organs have not yet lost power,
And life is still full and undiminished,
Now, now, struggle on,
rendering great help to yourself!
My friend, it is useless to try to dig a well
In a house that is already on fire!

In Shiva, who is the Lord of this Universe,
Or Vishnu, its soul, I see no difference,
But still, my love is for Him
Who wears the young moon on His forehead.

Oh when will that time come,
when in a beautiful full-moon night,
Sitting on the banks of some river,
And with calm, yet high notes,
repeating "Shiva! Shiva! Shiva!"
All my feelings will gush forth
through the adoring eyes.

Swami Sunirmalananda

Madhu:
The Sweet, Eternal Nectar

"Om madhu-vâtâ rtâyate. madhu ksharanti sindhavah. mâdhvirnah santu oshadhîh." [Rig Veda, 1.90.6]

This is the vision of the sage. *"The air is blowing sweetness, the rivers and oceans are flooding sweetness, and plants and trees are pouring out sweetness."* Tens of thousands of years ago, some Vedic *Rishi*, sitting somewhere in some remote forest, perhaps in the cold Himalaya, had a vision of the universe filled with sweetness, *madhu*. This was the transcendental vision — seeing beyond the manifestation. That is, seeing beyond what is apparent. Like the x-ray. It wasn't just a poetic imagination or a desire. Rather, it was one of the plain facts of the universe around.

Sweetness? *Madhu*? Nectarine sweetness in this world? It depends. There are several ways of looking at the manifested universe. For a child, it's all bright, beautiful, huge, colorful, and filled with surprises and joy. Even the truck picking up a waste container and dropping it back is a huge thing, a magic and a tremendous marvel for the child. For the elderly, on the other hand, who has tasted the bitter fruits of the world, it's all sorrow and suffering. That very "love" and "family life" which the youth seem to worship and crave for is for the elderly a plate of consolidated misery covered with a flowery lid. For *Advaitins*, and astrophysicists like Bernard Haisch, it's all consciousness with the universe being a simulation. For the dualist, it's God's creation. For the *yogis*, it's *prakriti's* dance to please the *purusha*.

There is another way of looking at things, which is to feel that the world is just inert matter. Objectively, this world is as it should be. We may call it sweet or bitter, depending on our own state of mind. When we are happy, the world is pleasant. When we have had some shocking experience, the world is bad. Though this is a good way of looking at the world, it is completely false. This is because the world is not merely inert, dead matter. It's brimming with life.

Pessimism due to a long life of toil and suffering, optimism because there's a long road to travel, indecisiveness because of mixed feelings about the world — all these are partial visions of the world. So what is the way?

Madhu-vâtâ rtâyate, the very air is brimming with blessed sweetness! This is the way. Changing the outlook about life and the world is the way. Perhaps you may think this is just another attempt at white-washing and trying to practice positive thinking. It is not.

The Vedas are eternal truths. They are neither past nor the distant future. *Veda* is in the present tense, in this moment. At this moment, the world is brimming with nectarine bliss, with sweetness, with divine blessedness. This is the fact. The sorrow, suffering, pain, war, bloodshed, etc., are all temporary coverings over the eternal truth of bliss.

Swami Vivekananda once commented about India. The slavery, abject poverty, disease, squalor etc., are all superficial. Behind and underneath all this is the glorious land of *tapas*, ready to do its part towards the good of the world. So with the world itself and the universe.

The question now is this: despite seeing misery all around, and being part of the miserable world, how can we brainwash ourselves into thinking that everything is sweet? The answer is not to limit our vision to what is apparent and passing. *Asatya* and *anitya* are the two qualifications of this world. And this in scientific Einsteinian language is relativity. Just imagine the scientist declaring as early as in 1915 that even time is not absolute, but relative! Everything is relative. Name, form, time, space, or spacetime, all are relative. So it's all unreal. This means that we should not limit our thinking, our lives, and our aspirations to just what is temporary and passing. Behind and beyond the temporary is the Permanent.

It is that Permanent, which is blowing sweetness with air, carrying sweet nectar with the waters, and is filling all life with sweetness. Just like we don't hang on to the wires but use the current that flows through them to light our homes, we should not hang on to the external but look for the sweetness which is flowing within.

Concentrating on that *Madhu*, nectarine sweetness, brings immortality. How and why? The external universe and the internal are made of the same material. The same air, filled with *madhu*, is keeping us alive also. Even as we respire, we inhale nectar. Our own Soul, the *Atman*, is the eternal source of that nectarine sweetness.

So whatever is apparently concrete, temporary, unreal, and impermanent, is acting as a block to the flow of that infinite sweetness. Instead of aiding the blockage, we should open up mentally and physically. To open up is just to accept that beyond the apparent miserable world there is that eternal universe of Consciousness, Divine bliss, and joy. Our own bodies are limited manifestations of our ego and ego-born past actions. They are changing and impermanent. We are not impermanent. We are that *Madhu* about which the *Vedic* Sage is declaring with tremendous force. We are beyond limitations.

This, then, is Vedanta. This is the truth of yogic science, or reality. Infinity, trying to think of itself as a limited, concrete, helpless, miserable "personality" is in delusion. Infinity, trying to remember its true divine nature, filled with *madhu* or immortal sweetness, is along the right path.

Swami Sunirmalananda is a sannyasin of the Ramakrishna Order, and the monk in-charge of the Vedanta Society of Holland. He is Swami Bhuteshanandaji's disciple. The Swami had the privilege of serving his guru for a decade before serving the Ramakrishna Order's centers in Brasil and Geneva.

◆ Annapurna Sarada

THE IMMEDIACY OF CONSCIOUSNESS
Revealed in Upanisadic Verses

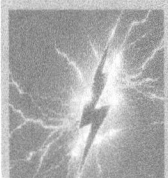

The ancient seers of India, via the practice of deep meditation, directly perceived an all-pervasive Reality that was the basis of everything – the world, the heavens, life, and living beings. This Realization did not belong to just one individual, but has become realized by countless others over millennia who followed the spiritual disciplines handed down from teacher to disciple and recorded in scriptures.

To perceive something directly removes all doubt about its veracity. For example, who can dispute their own existence? It is possible to deny everything – except the existence of the denier. This is the level of certainty a spiritual practitioner is eager for, whose aim is Self-Realization or God-Realization. The seers of India, ancient and modern, affirm that attaining either of these confers the direct perception that the Self and Brahman (ultimate Reality) are identical, or God alone *"exists everywhere and in everything, even here in this very life, mind, and body."* They left us a record of their direct perceptions in the Upanisads.

"All-pervading Reality" is perhaps a mysterious idea for some. What does "all-pervading" mean? Clay pervades a ceramic cup. Gold pervades a piece of jewelry. Neither cup nor jewelry would exist without the clay or the gold. This is one example. What is universally pervasive? Indian cosmology states that *akasha*, space/ether, pervades all objects, and at more subtle levels, there are *akashas* that pervade energy, mind, and intelligence. Beyond those *akashas*/ethers, is the *Chidakasha*, what the seers directly perceive as Consciousness/Reality, which is not contained by anything else. Swami Vivekananda once stated to a Western audience, *"God is not in the world; the world is in God."* And this means, logically, that God is Existence. This is also what is meant by "Immediate" in "the Immediacy of Consciousness." We are never separate or distinct from It. It is the Existence of our existence; the Consciousness of our consciousness; the Soul of our soul.

Most of us, distracted by daily concerns, do not spend time reflecting on such subtle ideas. However, those who do, exhibit a depth of peace and security that affects those in their presence. This alone should encourage us to spend quality time with these spiritual truths, transmitted by the seers via scriptures and qualified teachers of Vedanta. Then, we too can have unwavering peace of mind that will benefit our children, friends, coworkers, and communities. A poignant allegory is told to SRV children (and adults):

> Inside the blue-green ocean many kinds of colorful fish were swimming through the coral reefs, eating algae, hiding from bigger fish, raising little fish, and exploring all there was to see. A few were gathered together under a sea arch when another swam by and gurgled out to them,
>
> "Have you ever heard of something called 'water?'"
>
> "Water? What's that?" Bubbled most of the other fish.
>
> The first one gurgled back, "I'm not sure but it is supposed to be everywhere."
>
> A third fish splurted out, "I once heard about water from a very old fish a long time ago. He said there could be no life without it."
>
> An elder fish softly swirled in the coral, "I have never told anyfish before, but my grandfather left his school to look for water. Fish thought he had been stung by an urchin (that he was crazy). But we later heard from others that he had found it and called it the Source of Everything."
>
> "Hmmmm," bubbled the other fish, "We have never seen water so we can't believe this story."

Among several essential teachings, this story shows the necessity of direct perception – "seeing is believing." No one can know something for someone else; we have to know it for ourselves. Another point is that without assurance that the nature of Reality can be realized, few others will step onto the path that leads to direct experience. The fish are seeing water all the time and do not recognize it. Existence, Consciousness is our very nature, but we do not recognize It. We need guides, via the scriptures and in a qualified teacher. The Upanisads are the direct realizations of the *Aptas*. Swami Vivekananda struggled to find a good word in English for this term, and settled on "attained." An *Apta* is a being who has attained the realization that the Self and *Brahman* are one, and that being the case, they are incapable of deception or delusion, seeing the one Reality everywhere and in everything. The young Swami Vivekananda, searching ardently for the truth, asked Sri Ramakrishna if he had seen God. Sri Ramakrishna replied, *"yes, I see God more clearly than I see you. And you, too, can see Him."*

Because the Upanisads are the words of these *Aptas*, they are called *"Shruti,"* "to be heard." The great sage Vasishta states about the need of the scriptures: *"Trying to realize God without the help of the scriptures is like trying to grow crops only at night."* About the guru or teacher, he stated, *"The study of scripture without a guru for intellectual knowledge alone will lead one into ajnana, ignorance."* True Self-inquiry recognizes the words of guru and scriptures as the supreme authority. *"After the guru and the scriptures have been consulted, the quest for realization of the Atman begins in right earnest,"* that is, right effort for the purpose of direct experience, *Aparokshanubhuti*.

The Upanisads record countless statements on the immediacy of Consciousness. (Consciousness, Existence, Awareness, Reality, *Brahman, Atman* will be used interchangeably.) These awestruck, reverent, or matter of fact statements are there to guide and lift one's thinking consciousness to increasingly subtle perceptions. We should think to ourselves, "They attained direct experience, so it is possible for me too, if I follow in their footsteps." Even if we do not yet grasp this idea of all-pervasiveness, or the immediacy of Existence, we can begin to taste it with our minds by studying the Upanisadic record of the Indian *Rishis*. At the same time, we must keep in mind that words can only point to the experience but never fully describe it since it is beyond the scope of language. Still, how grateful we should be for their compassionate attempt to describe the indescribable.

Consciousness/Existence as the Ultimate Source of Phenomena, Penetrating All

Om purnam-adah purnam-idam
Purnat purnam udachyate
Purnasya purnam adaya
Purnam ev'avashisyate

That, the indivisible Brahman/Consciousness, is Infinite. This, the Universe of phenomena, is infinite in extension. This changing infinite has been projected from That unchanging Infinite. When this infinite merges in That Infinite, all that remains is Infinite.

(Yajur Veda Peace Chant, appearing in several Upanisads)

One of the primary practices of one following the path of knowledge is referred to as *neti-neti*, "not this, not this." The practitioner reasons that the tree is not God, the house is not God, the body and mind are not God. When he or she reaches the final stage of this practice it shifts into *iti-iti*, "all this, all this." Sri Ramakrishna used the metaphor of taking the brick stairs to the flat roof of an Indian house in 19th century Kolkata. A person leaves each step behind, because it is not the roof. Going step by step, rising closer and closer to the roof, a person negates the lowest to highest steps until they arrive on the roof. Then, looking at the roof, realizes it is made of the same bricks and mortar as the steps. Without undergoing a process of setting aside the changing for the Unchanging, which conditions the mind for subtle perceptions, one does not see the Essence (brick and mortar) inherent in all phenomena. The existence of phenomena is inseparable from Existence Itself.

Further, as the verse states, phenomena (names and forms, both material and conceptual) do not affect Existence in any way. This is one of the reasons that the teachers of Vedanta tell us that *Brahman* is the same in quantity and quality at all times; the difference is in manifestation. *"When the changing infinite merges back into the unchanging Infinite, all that remains is [the ever-unchanged] Infinite."* Thus, the rishi of this Peace Chant conveys that *Brahman* is the only Reality and Substance. What we see as phenomena ceaselessly arising (and falling, and arising) is the manifestation of *Brahman*, which remains unaffected throughout.

The following verse from the Mundaka Upanisad expresses another *rishi*'s direct perception that Consciousness/*Brahman* is inherent in all experiences. In our first verse, the emphasis was on recognizing an underlying substratum that was imminent in all we perceive. Shifting the focus to the experience of phenomena adds a new facet to the immediacy of Consciousness.

Avih sannihitam guha-charam nama
mahat padam atr'aitat samarpitam
ejat pranan nimisach cha yad etaj janatha sad asad-
varenyam param vijnanad yad varishtham prajanam

"This Brahman is the great support – manifesting through all experiences, existing very close, and moving in the cavity of the heart. All that move and breathe and wink are established in It. Know It – the cause of both the gross and the subtle, the adorable of all, the highest of being, the one above the understanding of creatures." Mundakopanisad, 2.2.1-2

With our minds habituated to thinking that internal experiences are caused by external phenomena, we overlook the unifying fact of Existence. Everything is saturated with a single Reality, connecting the experiencer and the experience itself – the one Source of both. One of the hallmarks of Indian thinking is the search for origins or the Source of everything. In deep meditation, the Indian seers realized that objects made of gross particles (atoms, molecules, etc.) are the result of subtle elements and forces, and

> "...words can only point to the experience but never fully describe it since it is beyond the scope of language. Still, how grateful we should be for their compassionate attempt to describe the indescribable."

that these, too, could be traced to even subtler causes (causal), and that all of these dissolved back into "the great Support," (*Brahman*/Existence) in nondual Realization. This became known as "involution," and is a mental discipline followed in Vedantic and Yogic meditation to arrive at the Source of Existence.

The practitioner can take this knowledge of the seers and use it to discriminate between the Real (the Great Support) and the unreal (everything that evolves and involves), and reject the universe of individual experience in favor of merging with ultimate Reality. That is one way. However, the *rishis*, illumined by direct experience of *Brahman*, show us the contentment, peace, and obvious bliss of directly perceiving that one Reality moment by moment in all experiences, without exception. Existence Itself, which is one without a second, is shining through all experiences – "closer than breathing" – unifying experience, experiencer, and that which is experienced

Consciousness as the Source of Perception

This next verse from the Kena Upanisad continues the thread of understanding, then recognizing, that Consciousness (Reality/Existence), is imminent in all experiences. We are never not experiencing It, we are simply not tuned into It.

Pratibodhaviditam matam amritatvam hi vindate
atmana vindite viryam vidyaya vindate'mrtam

Indeed, that one attains immortality, who intuits It [Atman/Brahman] in and through every modification of the mind. Through the Atman one obtains real strength, and through Knowledge, Immortality. Kena Upanisad, 2.4

In the process of perception, as Swami Vivekananda explains, each sense perception produces a wave or vibration in the "lake" of the mind (*chitta*). That wave is what we truly "see" and not the external object our senses encountered. The same holds true for memories, dreams, and other conceptual objects – they all produce a wave in the mind. This is what is being referred to as "modification of the mind." These waves get relayed to the intellect and ego aspects of the mind and then conveyed to the *Atman*, which is the only sentient principle in the entire process of perception.

Indivisible Consciousness, when appearing in the psychophysical being is called *Atman*. "*That one attains immortality (identification with one's deathless nature as Consciousness/Atman) who intuits*" this *Atman* even as the mind takes on modifications. The *Atman* is the witness of all these modifications; without It, there would be no perception. But most of us never identify ourselves with this Witness Self and instead identify with the mind and its modifications. The seer of this verse is exulting in intuiting the unchanging, eternal *Atman* in and through all these waves of the mind. Swami Sarvananda explains in his commentary: "*True strength is attained only when we feel certain that our real Self shall not in the least be affected, whatever might happen to our worldly interests. The realization of the Atman in every state of mind alone can give this strength unaccompanied by any fear of loss.*"

The famous Light Chant, which appears in numerous Upanisads, takes a direct approach to Consciousness as the one, Sentient principle that illumines the process of perception and everything else. Most of us are raised with the idea that light pertains only to external lights. Those who turn the mind inward perceive the self-effulgent Inner Light.

Om na tatra suryo bhati na chandratarkam
nema vidyuto bhanti kuto'yamagnih
tameva bhantamanubhati sarvam
tasya bhasa sarvamidam vibhati
There, within the indivisible Self of all living beings, the sun shines not, nor the moon, nor the stars, nor fire, nor lightning. That one Light shining, all else shines. By that Light all is illumined. - Katha Upanisad

Just as we would not use a flashlight to help us see the sun, the light of celestial orbs cannot reveal the Light of Consciousness, because that Itself is the source of our ability to see these lesser lights and all else. Swami Vivekananda, presenting this idea to Western audiences said, "*It is through the Self that you know anything. I see the chair; but to see the chair, I have first to perceive myself and then the chair. It is in and through the Self that the chair is perceived. It is in and through the Self that you are known to me, that the whole world is known to me....Take off the Self (Consciousness/Atman) and the whole universe vanishes.*" Complete Works of Swami Vivekananda, Practical Vedanta pt.1

Verses such as these are meant to be deeply contemplated, thereby making the mind more subtle and capable of intuiting the Light of Consciousness/Self. In the *Itihasa* (scriptural history) of India is the story of a dialog between a sage and a king millennia ago that leads the mind to shift its reliance on finite lights and look inward. The sage wants the king to trace the act of perception to its Source. In the process, the distinction between the true Seer/Witness and what is seen (the insentient lights and instruments of perception) is revealed:

The sage and the king:
Sage: By what light do you see?
King: I see by the light of the sun.
Sage: At night, by what light do you see?
King: I see by the light of the moon.
Sage: It is the new moon night,
by what light do you see?
King: I see by the light of the stars.
Sage: It is overcast. By what light do you see?
King: I see by the light of the fire.
Sage: Suppose you are blind, by what light do you see?
King: I see by the light of my senses.
Sage: Your outer senses are turned off in sleep,
by what light do you see?
King: I see by the light of my mind.
Sage: By what light does your mind see?

Most of us may be tempted to think that perception happens only while we are awake and using our senses and mental faculties, or having dreams. But what is going on when the mind is turned off in deep sleep? The seers and teachers of Vedanta tell us that in deep sleep we perceive both the absence of phenomena and the limited bliss that accompanies that state. What is it that lights the landscape of emptiness?

The Mandukyo Upanisad delineates four states of consciousness: waking, dream, sleep, and the "fourth" state that permeates and transcends the first three. This fourth state, *Turiya*, is explained mostly in the negative. It transcends cognition of anything "other," and thus is the single thread of "self-ness" that is with us as consciousness shifts between the three ordinary states. Piercing through the three common states of consciousness to the *Turiya* is Self-Realization. "*It is peace, it is bliss, it is nonduality. This is the Self, and it is to be realized.*"

"*The Fourth (Turiya), the wise say, is not inwardly cognitive, nor outwardly cognitive, nor cognitive both-wise; neither is it an indefinite mass of cognition, nor collective cognition, nor non-cognition. It is unseen, unrelated, inconceivable, uninferable, unimaginable, indescribable. It is the essence of the one self-cognition common to all states of consciousness**. *All phenomena cease in it. It is peace, it is bliss, it is nonduality. This is the Self, and it is to be realized.*" – Mundaka Upanisad, verse 7

**Ekatma-pratyaya-saram* – The essence of the one self-cognition common to all states of consciousness.

Annapurna Sarada lives in Waimea, Hawaii, where she continues her studies of Vedanta and Indian Religion and Philosophy with Babaji Bob Kindler, serves as the President and General Manager of SRV Associations, and offers live and on-line classes in the community, and for SRV Sangha.

Light Of Lights

This is a variation on the theme of the Light Chant written for children and set to music. It is an alternative to conventional children's rhymes.

Deep within our secret heart
That holds all worlds and skies,
Abides the Atman, ever bright,
The Light of every light,
The source of all our sight.

Before the sun can light the sky
Before the moon light beams
Before the stars twinkle and shine
Before the lightning gleams
The Light within our secret heart
Makes them all be seen.
Through Atman they are seen

The Atman shining all else shines,
It lights the sun and moon.
It lights the stars, the fireflies,
Volcanoes, bonfires too.
That one Light shining all else shines.
It's there in me and you.
It's there in me and you.

There within our secret heart
That holds all worlds and skies,
Is the Light that's ever True.
Atman, Light of lights -
The Light that never dies.
[the Light that ever shines]

Once There was a Contest for the Title of Infinite

Earth said, "I am infinite. Can you count all the grains of sand in me?"

Water said, "I am infinite. Can you swallow all my drops of water? Besides, I can easily cover you."

Fire said, "I am infinite. Don't you see me in all the stars? Besides, I can evaporate you."

Air said, "I am infinite. I am blowing everywhere. Besides, I can blow you out."

Space said, "I am infinite. All the planets and stars with all their air, fire, water, and earth rest in me! Without me, you would have no place to be!"

Mind said, "I am infinite. If I did not see you, would you exist?"

Atman, the inner Self said, "O mind, you disappear in deep sleep. Yet, I see you and everything in you. I am formless but all forms are in Me. I am Infinite."

◆ Anurag Neal Aronowitz

DEHYPNOTIZING THE MIND WITH VEDANTA
Removing False Coverings Over the Self

What is the crux of the spiritual predicament of most people navigating their way through earthly existence? The experience of the individual soul is of one typically ensnared in a labyrinth of limited consciousness, where an incessant stream of thoughts forms an intricate web of confusion, doubt, and fear. This metaphysical problem, according to Vedanta, lies at the heart of the human predicament. Vedanta precisely pinpoints our situation as a forgetfulness of our real nature. We think that we are people subject to birth and death, with a beginning and an end. The present malady stems from this misidentification, where a false ego dominates, leading to a self-centered life. This is by no means a natural condition. It is an aberration, unworthy of this rare privilege of precious human birth with its potential for the realization of our true infinite being and ultimately our union and identification with *Brahman*.

This misguided awareness of who and what we are becomes the root cause of conflicts, disharmony, and negativity in our lives. The unfortunate truth behind this bondage of earthly life is not external, but is made up by our own self. It is an inner state of becoming deprived of true awareness, enslaved by a deluded consciousness, dominated by a false ego, accompanied and complicated by ignorance and selfishness.

Swami Vivekananda frequently explained this misunderstanding by likening it to a form of hypnosis. In a lecture and discussion at Harvard University he was asked, "...do you know of any people who have made any study of the principles of self-hypnotism, which they undoubtedly practiced to a great extent in ancient India, and what has been recently stated and practiced in that study? Of course, you do not have it so much in modern India."

Swamiji answered, *"What you call hypnotism in the West is only a part of the real thing. The Hindus call it self-hypnotization. They say you are hypnotized already, and that you should get out of it and de-hypnotize yourself.*

"There the sun cannot illumine, nor the moon, nor the stars; the flash of lightning cannot illumine That; what to speak of this mortal fire! That shining, everything else shines' (Katha Upanishad, II ii. 15).

"That is not hypnotization, but de-hypnotization. We say that every other religion that preaches these things as real is practicing a form of hypnotism. It is the Advaitist alone that does not care to be hypnotized. His is the only system that understands that hypnotism comes with every form of dualism. But the Advaitist says, throw away even the Vedas, throw away even the Personal God, throw away even the universe, throw away even your own body and mind, and let nothing remain in order to get rid of hypnotism perfect. From where the mind comes back with speech, being unable to reach, knowing the Bliss of Brahman, no more is fear. That is de-hypnotization.

"I have neither vice nor virtue, nor misery nor happiness; I care neither for the Vedas nor sacrifices nor ceremonies; I am neither food nor eating nor eater, for I am Existence Absolute, Knowledge Absolute, Bliss Absolute; I am He, I am He.'

"We know all about hypnotism. We have a psychology which the West is just beginning to know, but not yet adequately, I am sorry to say."

He also addressed this phenomenon with the Hindus in India as recorded in a talk found in the book, Lectures From Colombo to Almora:

"Let us proclaim to every soul, 'Arise, awake and stop not till the goal is reached.' Arise, Awake from hypnotism of this weakness. None is really weak; the soul is infinite, omnipotent and omniscient. Stand up, assert yourself, proclaim the God within you, do not deny him! Too much of inactivity, too much of weakness, too much of hypnotism, has been & is upon our race. O ye modern Hindus, de-hypnotize yourselves. The way to do that is found in your own sacred books. Teach yourself, teach everyone his real nature, call upon the sleeping soul and see how it awakes. Power will come, glory will come, goodness will come, purity will come, everything that is excellent will come when this sleeping soul is roused to self-conscious activity."

Vedanta, Voice of Freedom

This stirring Vedantic message, therefore, is a resounding call to freedom, urging individuals to recognize and embrace their birthright. The body, the senses, the mind, the intellect, and even the ego all lack true freedom. True liberation centers around a singular entity that comprehends all — the infinite *Atman*, our true nature. It beckons individuals to acknowledge their status and identity as the eternal Now, the Unborn, undying Self, rather than being confined to the known, the non-self, the object.

In the pursuit of understanding the true Self within, various contenders present themselves as potential embodiments of selfhood. The body, the senses, the mind, and the intellect, all lay claim to being the Self, yet a closer examination reveals this fallacy.

The non-dual wisdom of Vedanta, transmitted from time immemorial via the luminaries of ancient India, cuts through the profound question as to who and what we are, and conversely what we are not. This reality beckons individuals to embark on a profound journey of investigation, prompting the question as to where one should look for this hidden truth. As Swamiji suggested, the way to do this is found in the rich storehouse of sacred teachings. The Upanishads, the Bhagavad Gita, and Brahma Sutras contain and reveal the sacred knowledge and wisdom of the Atman, hidden within everyone and which is veiled by the mind-body complex. These revealed scriptures, particularly when transmitted from an illumined teacher or *Guru*, effectively and systematically impart the knowledge (*Brahma-vidya*) and methodology to the qualified student who desires freedom, referred to in Sanskrit as "*Mumukshutvam*," the longing for liberation.

Transmitted in such a manner, from qualified teacher to qualified student, Vedanta is truly life-transforming. The aspirant progresses through hearing (*Shravana*), contemplating (*Manana*), and meditating (*Nididhyasanam*) on the truth as revealed by the scriptures and teacher. *Nididhyasanam* is a particularly crucial step. Constant absorption in the teachings regarding the nondual Brahman, combined with firm determination for its realization, will lead to the transcendence of identification with body, senses, mind, and ego. Vigilance is required as well. Vedanta, through *Mahavakyas* or great statements such as *Tat Tvam Asi*, or Thou Art That, dispels the notion that these affirmations are mere self-hypnosis. Instead, it contends that individuals have been hypnotized into false identities — believing themselves to be merely the body, a human being with a specific identity tethered to familial, cultural, and national affiliations. The journey of de-hypnotization, therefore, is an unraveling of these misconceptions accumulated through countless lifetimes of erroneous thinking.

The spiritual journey is fraught with potential risks of backsliding into false identification. A famous warning is found in the Katha Upanishad: *"Arise! Awake! Approach the great ones and learn from them. Like the sharp edge of a razor is that path, so the wise say – hard to tread, and difficult to cross."*

can extend this metaphor to describe how the *jiva*, or individual self, bound by time, space, and causation, is superimposed on the ever-free, never-bound *Atman*.

Apavada is the systematic method of correcting, through negation, this false notion, and reestablishing the truth of our true nature. By negating the attributes of the illusory snake, the true nature of the rope is revealed. Likewise, by negating the attributes of the limited self, the true nature of the *Atman* is revealed. The process of "de-superimposition" involves overcoming this ignorance, or *ajnana*. The hypnotic spell of a limited relative existence is overcome. *Apavada* is the antidote for *Adyaropa*.

Vedanta contains a rich trove of innumerable inspiring teachings and methods to gain knowledge of the Self. Embarking on this profound journey, we encounter the concept of the Five *Koshas*, or sheaths, which intricately cover and veil the true essence of the *Atman*. They can be pictured as layers or coverings, enveloping our innermost self. These sheaths play a pivotal role in obscuring the sublime reality of *Atman*.

The outermost layer is the *annamayakosa*, the gross physical sheath, i.e., our tangible body composed of flesh, bones, and

> "...individuals have been hypnotized into false identities — believing themselves to be merely the body, a human being with a specific identity tethered to familial, cultural, and national affiliations. The journey of de-hypnotization, therefore, is an unraveling of these misconceptions accumulated through countless lifetimes of erroneous thinking."

The Upanishads reveal that *Brahman*, or Consciousness, is the ultimate reality and our true being. Receiving and integrating the knowledge of the Self, the student can begin to recognize and overcome the ignorance caused by the impurities of the mind. This is a message proclaiming that freedom is the birthright of every individual. The truth is that the individual self is inherently one with the great Self. *Atman* and *Brahman* are one. A deep study of these precious teachings can inspire the mind, previously bound under the hypnotic spell of finitude, to cognize its eternal infinite nature, free from limitations. The body, senses, mind, and ego are not free. Only the infinite *Atman*, our true nature, embodies this freedom. Vedanta sheds light on the understanding of this truth via the teachings of false superimposition known as *Adhyaropa* and *Apavada*, which describe the cause of this distorted perception of reality.

Vedanta posits that all beings abide as Pure Consciousness and Pure Bliss — *Sat-Chit-Ananda*. Yet, the experience of the universe as inert, as well as the illusion of separateness, arise due to false mental and intellectual superimposition. Swami Vivekananda elucidates this by likening it to when the mother-of-pearl (the shiny inside of a shell) is mistaken for pure silver. The analogy illustrates the superimposition of the unreal (*mithya*) on the real (*satyam*). A relative existence is wholly dependent upon a real one.

Adhyaropa defines this confounding superimposition by which something is misperceived, and the qualities of one thing are confused with another. The famous illustration of misperceiving a rope appearing to be a snake is due to this *adhyaropa*. Likewise, we

blood. Its a masterpiece of nature, but the wise recognize it as the nonself. Among other problems, identifying solely with the body keeps one entangled in the illusion of separation, hindering the experience of blissful freedom.

Moving inward, we encounter the *pranamayakosha*, the sheath of *Prana*, the subtle force that propels us into action. However, it is limited and insentient, often mistaken for the *Atman* by beginning aspirants. The journey to Self-realization involves detaching from this sheath through discernment and discrimination, along with the guidance of an illumined preceptor.

Deeper still is the *manomayakosha*, the mental sheath, where the mind is mesmerized with desires, experiences the world's diversity, and succumbs to pleasure and pain. Yet it, too, is not the *Atman*. Its transient nature, subject to change and characterized by duality, cannot be the Eternal Self.

Beyond the mental realm lies the *vijnanamayakosa*, the sheath of intelligence, *Buddhi*, reflecting pure Consciousness. This reflective intelligence, called the *Jiva*, is entangled in the *karmic* play of good and evil actions. Recognizing the limitations of this sheath is a crucial step towards Self-realization.

The most subtle layer is the *anandamayakosa*, the sheath of bliss, a finer sheath close to *Atman*, but still a product of ignorance. It is essential not to mistake this veiled bliss for the supreme Bliss of *Atman/Brahman*. Here the student treads the very delicate path of discernment, carefully distinguishing between the temporary ecstasy of the ego, and the eternal Bliss (*ananda*) inherent in the *Atman*.

> "Through discrimination and detachment, and the purification of mind gained through the knowledge imparted by the scriptures and the *Guru*, the seeker sheds identification with the *Koshas* and all other coverings. In this process, the true glory of the *Atman*, unobstructed and eternal, is revealed."

It is crucial to understand that these five sheaths lack absolute reality. Their mistakenly perceived reality stems from the *Atman* being their substratum. They act as veils, momentarily obscuring the brilliance of *Atman*. Through discrimination (*viveka*) and detachment (*vairagya*), and the purification of mind gained through the knowledge imparted by the scriptures and the *Guru*, the seeker sheds identification with the *Koshas* and all other coverings. In this process, the true glory of the *Atman*, unobstructed and eternal, is revealed.

The Positive Effect of Negation

As the spiritual aspirant proceeds to negate the five sheaths, namely body, energy, mind, intelligence, and ego, the hypnotic spell of false superimposition subsides. The radiant reality of the *Atman* then emerges. Additionally, unwanted negativities such as fear, grief, sorrow, and death dissipate, making way for a very welcome clarity leading to eternal peace and bliss. Vedanta, with its profound ignorance-destroying, mind de-hypnotizing wisdom, beckons the seeker to uncover these mentally superimposed layers, break the bonds of the world of relativity, and embrace the supreme knowledge embedded within the core of the eternal Self, *Atman*.

In Conclusion

In conclusion, the exploration of Vedanta's teachings related to de-hypnotizing the mind from the intricacies of misidentification, leads us on a profound journey of self-discovery and liberation. As the seeker contemplates the teachings of Vedanta, the recognition of the eternal *Atman* guides us toward the ultimate realization of our innate divinity, and the liberation from the illusions that bind us.

Anurag Neal Aronowitz is the Vice-President of SRV Associations and a student of Vedanta for over thirty years. He is an artist and designer, and lives in Portland, Oregon.

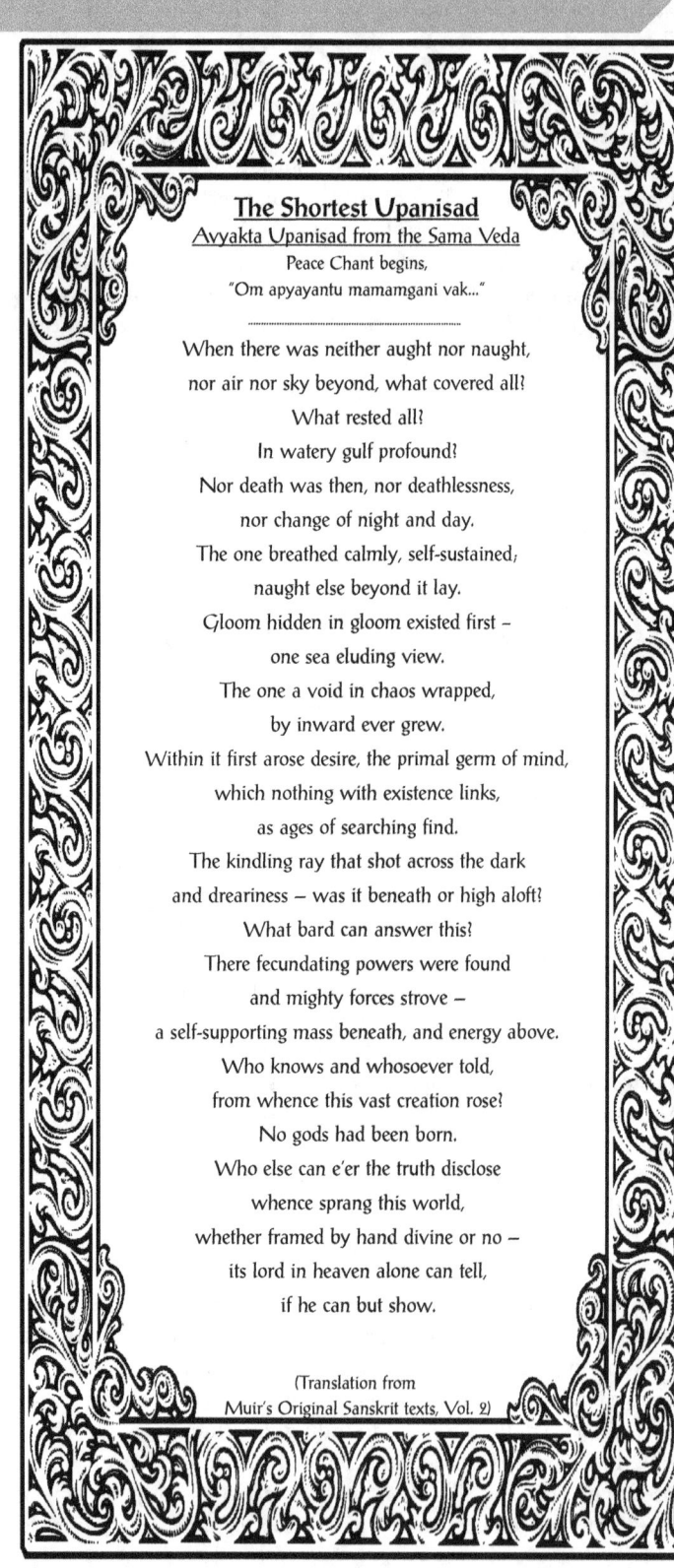

The Shortest Upanisad
Avyakta Upanisad from the Sama Veda
Peace Chant begins,
"Om apyayantu mamamgani vak..."

When there was neither aught nor naught,
nor air nor sky beyond, what covered all?
What rested all?
In watery gulf profound?
Nor death was then, nor deathlessness,
nor change of night and day.
The one breathed calmly, self-sustained;
naught else beyond it lay.
Gloom hidden in gloom existed first –
one sea eluding view.
The one a void in chaos wrapped,
by inward ever grew.
Within it first arose desire, the primal germ of mind,
which nothing with existence links,
as ages of searching find.
The kindling ray that shot across the dark
and dreariness – was it beneath or high aloft?
What bard can answer this?
There fecundating powers were found
and mighty forces strove –
a self-supporting mass beneath, and energy above.
Who knows and whosoever told,
from whence this vast creation rose?
No gods had been born.
Who else can e'er the truth disclose
whence sprang this world,
whether framed by hand divine or no –
its lord in heaven alone can tell,
if he can but show.

(Translation from
Muir's Original Sanskrit texts, Vol. 2)

Alexander Hixon

NONDUAL POLYTHEISTIC PLURALISM
Religions As Independent Currents & Tides in One Planetary Ocean

The deity Manjusri appeared in dreamvision to the great Buddhist teacher Atisa, revealing to him that the school of *prasangika madhyamika* contained the fullest expression of truth. This is a good example of the peculiar functioning of *tantric*, or nondual, theism: the deity appears and reveals a truth in which all concept of deity is undercut. Due in some measure to the vigor of Atisa (and the grace of Manjusri), the *prasangika madhyamika* became the universal basis of Tibetan Buddhism. One could translate *prasangika* as "avoidance" the avoidance of assertion through the discovery of the void or non-binding nature of any particular assertion. Leaving aside the fact that followers of the *prasangika madhyamika* often become strangely assertive, the *prasangika* approach provides a void basis for the free pluralism of tantric theistic practice. When there can be no binding system of assertions, there is no limit to the number and nature of revelatory deities which can flourish in emptiness without holding rival ontological claims; the function of these deities, which are nonentities, is to reveal the unbound, free-form nature of all form, to reveal truth. The *vajrayana*, or way of tantra, is theistic and pluralistic. Theism and pluralism are the two issues we want to discuss briefly.

Nonduality in Essence

Among the forms of theism, tantric theism is indeed somewhat unconventional because it springs out of the nondual insight which clearly recognizes no differences in essence between worshipper and worshipped. But it is not merely a provisional theism, cleverly designed to destroy itself, because the deities do not become obsolete to enlightened practitioners. Atisa did not consider Manjusri simply as his own mind revealing to him the truth of *prasangika madhyamika*. Manjusri is undoubtedly buddha-mind, but so is the Crab Nebula, and as no astronomer considers this giant cluster of stars a fiction or projection of his own mind, in the same sense, no tantric practitioner considers his chosen deity a fiction or projection of his own mind. Actually, it is the deities who project us, rather than we who project the deities.

Also, the tantric practitioner does not seek to merge with the deity in a monistic sense. There is a proud exhilaration of nonduality of essence between practitioner and deity, but the reverential relationship with the deity is maintained and deepened. The deity is not a cardboard container for the nectar of nondual insight or bliss-void, to be thrown away after the nectar is consumed. The deity is a permanent expression of insight, emptiness, and bliss. Actually, it is the practitioner who is a cardboard container, whose body and mind are eventually thrown away in death. The tantric experience of theistic relationship in the minds of nondualists is perhaps best expressed by the symbol of sexual union. The playful twoness is an essential expression of the nondual bliss. But the image of biological human sexuality is not entirely apt because it brings together two elements, the male and the female, into ecstatic union, whereas the Great Bliss of tantra is not a joining together but the discovery of an innate, natural nonduality which playfully projects from itself the elements of male and female, worshipper and worshipped. The play does not create the nonduality; the nonduality generates the play. Theism is the play between worshipper and worshipped, seeker and sought; many spiritual traditions accept the imagery of lover and beloved – though often not in the overtly sexual mode — as the most accurate description of the play. For advanced practitioners, this play deepens and intensifies. What becomes realized cannot be put into words. To state it as a philosophical doctrine of nondualism, qualified nondualism, or dualism, and then to argue about it, is somewhat beside the point. We can only say that intimacy intensifies to the point of identity, steps back to enjoy itself, and then reintensifies in a kind of endless sexual rhythm. This structure and rhythm can be discerned even in such an overtly nontheistic atmosphere as zen koan practice. The zen master Hakuin had five ecstatic great enlightenment experiences in this loveplay with the truth. Even in the absence of a formal deity, the ecstatic spiritual play which is theism manifests itself, not abstractly through concepts, but concretely as divinehuman energies. The *guru, lama, roshi* or *tzaddik* often takes the place of a transcendent deity-form as the beloved. All worshippers or seekers (those of Dionysus, Christ, Kali, Allah, Bodhi, Brahman, Tao, Torah and on and on) are channels for the theistic playfulness of the truth, which is itself void of structure, yet full of energy.

Tantric Pluralism

This brings us to the issue of tantric pluralism. Countless sadhanas or formal worship of deities are recorded side by side in the Buddhist *sadhanamala*, or "garland of *sadhanas.*" There is no sense that the practice of one deity is fundamentally superior or contradictory to that of another, yet at the same time, there is a fierce mood of total dedication of one's energy to the particular *sadhana* in which one is engaged. The fullness and accuracy of practice is considered a life-and-death matter; partial and casual experimentation with several *sadhanas*, serially or simultaneously, would be unthinkable for the serious tantric practitioner. Thus tantric pluralism is very far from the uninformed, unprepared-for, uncommitted, and therefore irresponsible experimentation with various spiritual practices which are coming into fashion in the West today as a kind of cross-cultural theater of religious liberalism. But distortions of the pluralistic approach should not blind us to its essential truth. Tantric pluralism is based on the *prasangika madhyamika*: if no formulation of the Real is accepted as accurate (simply because of its very nature as formula), then countless formulations can be freely allowed to exist side by side as vehicles for the awakening to the Real. One does not awaken to the non-formulatability of the Real by simply and abstractly contemplating the assertion of its non-formulatability (which is itself nothing but another formulation). One realizes nonformulatability concretely by penetrating deeper and deeper into one or more particular formulations, by living them with total intensity.

A Garland of Sadhanas

Why not regard all the authentic spiritual traditions of the planet as a *sadhanamala*, a gigantic garland of *sadhanas*? Each of these *sadhanas*, when undertaken with total dedication and thorough preparation, leads to an overtly or covertly nondual intimacy

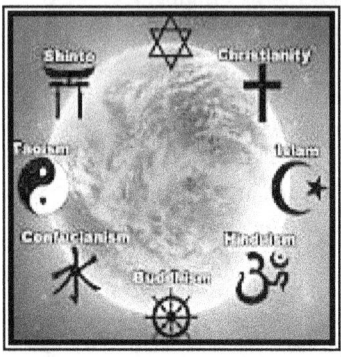

with a particular mode of playfulness, energy-current, or deity-form of reality itself, if one has the courage and strength to pursue the *sadhana* to its root or to surrender to it with complete abandon, rather than adopting the practice in a mild, conventional manner.

Sadhanas are like children. One can have several children, fully loving and nurturing each one; in fact, an only-child does not always prosper psychologically. But here we must point out a common error in the understanding of spiritual pluralism. Religious traditions do not "say the same thing in different languages." They each say something unique. Nor do the spiritual exercises of the various traditions "lead to the same ultimate experience." Enlightened persons from different streams of spiritual practice do not readily agree on the nature of realization. Each enlightenment is a unique flowering of truth. Pluralism goes right down to the root; it is radical pluralism. All spiritual practices are independent currents or tides in one planetary ocean. The Gulf Stream is not equivalent to or interchangeable with some current in the Indian Ocean or some tide along the coast of Japan.

Because of the tremendous development of planetary communications, radical spiritual pluralism is emerging now for the first time in the history of human civilizations as a concrete cultural possibility. But if it emerges simply on the cultural plane, it becomes merely a form of diplomacy or theater, not a transforming realization of nonduality. Pluralism must discover its own spiritual authenticity, and this authenticity is available through the *prasangika madhyamika* and the practice of tantra (but not exclusively there; the potentiality for it exists in each spiritual current). The fact that Indian culture has provided useful initial modes for spiritual pluralism can be seen as a confirmation of the potency of tantric pluralism, because, as Trungpa Rinpoche and other tantric practitioners and scholars have observed, there is little spiritual practice on the Indian subcontinent which has not been subtly imbued with tantric influences. On the Indian subcontinent religious paths are indeed regarded as a *sadhanamala*, although bitter quarreling among adherents of the various sects is also prevalent. We have to carry this attitude of the garland of *sadhanas* further and develop it more consciously, dissolving the idea that Christianity and Islam, Hinduism, and Buddhism are solid, mutually exclusive entities; religions are not solid entities, any more than cultures or nations are. When the nondual insight into emptiness has revealed the void, non-obstructing nature of all categories, then various cultural, philosophical, and religious forms can stay in play, now transparent and therefore free from mutual antagonism.

The countless deity-forms are not to be discarded after they are discovered to be innately transparent to the formless truth. A harmonious polycultural world-view can be created with these transparent forms — a polytheism which is nondual. This is the *vajra* path as it manifests in the planetary age, moving in new cultural directions with the same nondual insight and with the same deities, such as the marvelous *Mahakala-Mahakali*, who appear revealing a truth in which various spiritual traditions flourish even as the very concept of separate traditions is undercut.

Lex Hixon received his Ph.D. in World Religions from Columbia University in 1976. From about 1971 to the late 80's he conducted a weekly radio show in New York City called "In The Spirit," interviewing spiritual teachers from around the world. In the years that followed he entered into deep, serious study and practice of several of the world's religious traditions, eventually becoming a masterful teacher in some of them — including the Western chapter of the Jerrahi Order of Istanbul with its several tekkas. Among his books are Great Swan, Mother of the Universe, Heart of the Koran, Atom from the Sun of Knowledge, Mother of the Buddhas, and Living Buddha Zen. For the In The Spirit interreligious interviews Series information inquire at: www.srv.org

REV. KOSHO FINCH ◆

THE EMBODIED PRACTICE OF SHINGON
& The Direct Benefits of Pilgrimage

I often say that everyone has heard of Zen, but almost no one has heard of Shingon. Somehow this older Buddhist lineage remains largely obscured outside Japan. Perhaps due to its perch in the mountains far from the glittering lights of cities like Tokyo, Shingon remains lesser known among the ancient Japanese Buddhist traditions. I invite you to continue reading so that I might introduce you to one of the most influential Buddhist schools in Japan, one that has sustained people from the countryside to the palace, and across time, through to Japanese immigrants to Hawaii and the mainland United States who established mnay temples as they immigrated.

First, the name of this school. Zen is familiar, its name is the translation of "meditation," *dhyana* in Sanskrit, and when translated into Chinese, is *Chan* 禪, which pronounced in Japanese, becomes *Zen*. The school is named for its central practice method, meditation. Shingon, is similarly named for its central practice method, *mantra*. When translated into Chinese, *mantra* becomes, 真言, *zhenyán*, which is pronounced *Shingon*, in Japanese. This tradition was introduced to Japan during its classical period, as it imported religion, philosophy, and government systems from China. In the late 700's a young man was born who would go on to take the Buddhist name, Kukai. He would go on to establish the Shingon school and remake the Buddhist landscape there, and have a lasting influence on art, poetry, calligraphy, and religious thinking.

In many ways Kukai's origin story may remind readers of the biography of a Silicon Valley tech entrepreneur. Having become disillusioned in college by the promise of a secure position in government, Kukai left school and pursued a different dream. His interests turned philosophical having encountered the Buddha's teaching. During Kukai's time, rather than established universities, youth from families with means were sent to private tutors to prepare them in a classical education. The education was largely modeled on the Chinese classical education system, where focus was on the Four Books, and Five Classics, specifically core Confucian texts, and other fundamental texts of Chinese antiquity. By all accounts Kukai excelled at his studies. His writings remain largely untranslated in part due to the numerous historical and literary references that complicate their understanding for modern audiences. His calligraphy remains a model for calligraphic studies.

After leaving school, Kukai traveled around Japan studying with various Buddhist teachers, and making the Japanese countryside and mountains his place of practice. For ten years he perfected himself in nature. His travels and practice on the Japanese island of Shikoku became a pilgrimage route that all but defines an entire island of the Japanese archipelago. In 2014, the island celebrated the 1,200-year anniversary of this pilgrimage route. The 750 mile route traverses mountains and cities and connects 88 temples that commemorate significant aspects of Kukai's life. It is estimated that approximately 150,000 people make the journey each year, retracing Kukai's path physical and spiritually.

The Shikoku pilgrimage represents a type of embodied practice that has endured across time, and which represents a key feature of Shingon. Like the Camino de Santiago, pilgrims walk portions, or the entirety of the route. In modern times pilgrims may travel between the temples by car or bus. The route is divided into four 道場, *dojo*. The term *dojo* is most often associated with martial arts practice, but these sacred places, or literally "places of enlightenment," each represent a stage in the journey of the spiritual seeker. Each *dojo* is today represented by the four prefectures of the island. The pilgrim begins in the *Dojo* of Awakening Faith, moving to the *Dojo* of Religious Discipline, then to the *Dojo* of Enlightenment, and completing the journey at temple 88 in the *Dojo* of *Nirvana*. All along the way, the pilgrims carry a special walking staff that is symbolic of Kukai accompanying them. Either on the staff, their pilgrims hat, or clothing, will be written the reminder, 同行二人, *dogyo ninin*, "two people practicing together," an affirmation that the pilgrim is accompanied by Kukai on their journey. In 2014, the pilgrimage route was featured in the PBS docuseries, Sacred Journeys.

In the early 800's, Kukai made the arduous journey to China by sea. He was motivated to take this journey to find a teacher who specialized in a lineage not yet transmitted to Japan. Kukai would successfully make this journey and return as the lineage holder of the school that would become Shingon. Shingon is variously described as Tantra, Esoteric Buddhism, or 密教 *Mikkyo*, secret teaching. The idea of "secret" is often misunderstood when presented in Western languages. It isn't that the teachings are secret, as previously mentioned countless people engage with this lineage through pilgrimage, and Japanese immigrants established temples in the United States, which continue to operate to this day. Rather, "secret" here refers to a distinction between esoteric and exoteric. Kukai, upon his return to Japan, wrote extensively about this distinction. His intent was to turn our gaze inward, and to assist us in reading scripture more deeply.

The Buddhist cannon is vast. The Buddha taught for over 40 years. His teachings, rules for the monastic community, and the resulting commentaries or explanatory treatises, fill countless volumes. As the Buddha's teaching spread to East Asia, additional commentarial literature was added. Kukai noted that cannon contained two general categories of teaching, one is the exoteric, that which can be understood through reading. Such works include ethical teaching, meditation instruction, Buddhist psychology, and the like. Another level of teaching is esoteric, or hidden, because it represents the inner experience of the Buddha or the practitioner.

For example, in the pilgrimage I discussed above, we can get an idea of the length of the trail, the items carried, or the stops along the way. No matter how gifted the writer or cinematographer, the experience of the pilgrimage, the effort, the scent of incense, the feeling of other pilgrims reciting prayers, eludes us. The experience remains hidden, secret, until we too engage ourselves with it.

Shingon is better explained as a practice layer atop the Buddhist teaching. This sometimes makes explanations challenging as the practices sit atop established teachings. In many ways the years of Kukai studying and perfecting himself in the wilds of Shikoku Island, are reflected in practices and instructions that assume students have studied the underlying texts and methods. The Western popularization of silent sitting meditation practice as representative of East Asian spiritual traditions, can work to

symbol, *mantra*, or a specific Buddha.

Pilgrimage in Shingon borrows the ritual meditation form. There is a set etiquette and manners for entering the temple, performing ablutions, offering of incense, and recitation of *mantras*. Throughout the pilgrimage, whether one visits a single temple or completes the entire pilgrimage route, the pilgrim will encounter お接待, *Osettai*, or the giving of alms to pilgrims.

Adapted from the Indian custom of giving alms to wandering ascetics, everyone on the pilgrimage path becomes transformed into one worthy of receiving alms. Residents of Shikoku Island symbolically support pilgrims by offering all manner of food, drink, and hospitality. In this way, the giver takes part in the pilgrimage of each person they make offering to. The entire community of residents and pilgrims become interwoven in spiritual practice. Each temple along the pilgrimage offers the pilgrim the opportunity to collect a stamp and hand written calligraphy from that temple, which is added to the pilgrims 納経帳 *nokyo-cho* book. This book, filled with the stamps and names of each temple, becomes a treasured memory of the pilgrim's journey.

> "...the meditation practices have a set sequence. Entering into, engaging in, and exiting from the meditative state has specific steps that are repeated, that thereby become ritualized. Another level of understanding ritual meditation involves practice of visualization of the individual's union with the object of meditation, whether that is a symbol, mantra, or a specific Buddha."

obscure the larger spiritual landscape in the Buddhist world. Practice is more often found in the daily routine of offering flowers, incense, tending shrines and temples, and of course, pilgrimage.

Kukai famously announced the idea, 即身成佛, *sokushin jobutsu*, or attaining enlightenment with this very body. As with many of Kukai's writings, this idea can be understood in several ways. First, in response to the idea prominent during Kukai's time, one did not have to practice for innumerable eons, but rather could attain enlightenment in the present body. The idea can also be understood as a reinterpreting the existing Mahayana Buddhist idea of inherent enlightenment, or Buddha-nature. In this way, Buddhist practice works to uncover the individual's original enlightened nature. The right combination of experiences and practices, can combine to awaken a person to this inner truth.

A key feature of Shingon is ritual meditation. Again, this can be understood in several ways. One way is that the meditation practices have a set sequence. The entering into, engaging in, and exiting from the meditative state, have specific steps that are repeated, that thereby become ritualized. Another level of understanding ritual meditation involves practices of visualization of the individual's union with the object of meditation, whether that is a

Kukai was granted the mountain known as 高野山 Koyasan, or Mount Koya, to establish a monastic complex. The mountain is the physical and spiritual home of Shingon Buddhism. It is home to hundreds of temples, the main seminary, university, museum, and innumerable national treasures. To this day it remains a place of pilgrimage, study, and practice. In 2004, the United Nations named it a UNESCO World Heritage site. The mountain is part of a historical pilgrimage route connecting ancient Shinto and Buddhist sites in Japan. Most pilgrims undertaking the Shikoku pilgrimage begin and end their pilgrimage on the mountain, paying their respects at Kukai's mausoleum on the mountain.

This meditation brings all the elements of Shingon practice together. The landscape is transformed into a *mandala* through which the pilgrim transits on their way to spiritual awakening. Each step is made together with Kukai, intoning *mantras*, reciting the core *sutras* of Buddhist wisdom, and joining hands in prayer at countless temples along the way. The same practice is reenacted daily at temples in miniature, with practitioners offering incense, joining hands in deep respect, and engaging in the very same prayers.

Kukai is much beloved in Japan due to his Buddhist innovations and social improvements. Until modern times, the Japanese syllabary was taught through a poem attributed to him, such was his fame. Kukai established the first public school in Japan, ensuring that children could attend tuition free. He is known for bringing medical and engineering knowledge from China that improved the lives of people. While Kukai introduced sophisticated Buddhist philosophical writings to Japan, and a new system of artistic religious expression with *mandalas* and tantric deities, he also brought Buddhist practice out of the monastery and to the people directly. This indelible impact is celebrated and remembered in a variety of ways to this day.

then work to see the deeper meanings that may have been hidden to us previously.

> "Pilgrimage can be transformative and life altering. It can be a journey of a lifetime. It can also be something we do in our local community. We can give alms literally or symbolically to those in need. We can also find ways to embody our practice more deeply. When we read scripture, we can then work to see the deeper meanings that may have been hidden to us previously."

The Shikoku pilgrimage is such an integral part of Shingon practice, that the pilgrimage is often reenacted in local temples for those unable to undertake the pilgrimage. In this practice, sand from each of the 88 temples is arranged before a scroll. Each temple along the 88 temples pilgrimage enshrines a different statute of a Buddha or Boddhisatva. Scrolls bearing the image of each 本尊 *Honzon*, the main image of that temple, is arranged in the temple halls. Several Shingon temples in Hawaii have permanent miniature pilgrimage routes established on the temple grounds. On Kauai, for example, the Shingon temple there includes a miniature version of the Shikoku pilgrimage constructed from military surplus remaining on the island following the end of the second world war. Today, each station includes a small statute of the *Honzon* of each of the 88 temples of the pilgrimage. Locals can reenact the pilgrimage locally each year as part of a special temple celebration. With each station containing the sands from the temples in Japan, local pilgrims can still traverse the sacred landscape.

During the COVID-19 pandemic, many of us went to work and school online. For many, that online-connected world continued. That is also true for the temple; we took our classes, services, and social meetings online. Following the height of the pandemic we continue to offer an online option and welcome the friends we've made around the world. Yet pilgrimage is a teaching that we have a deep human need to connect to, to move, and to fully experience the practice of with others in the world. Even in ancient times, movement was imperative for transformation. Removing oneself from the familiar landscape, the effort required, the sacrifices made to take time away. All have an invaluable transformative effect.

No matter how you express your spiritual practice, I offer you some inspiration from the Shikoku pilgrimage. Pilgrimage can be transformative and life altering. It can be a journey of a lifetime. It can also be something we do in our local community. We can give alms literally or symbolically to those in need. We can find ways to embody our practice more deeply. When we read scripture, we can

We live in a sacred landscape no matter where we are, it only takes our willingness to see it as sacred to transform it. While Kukai's teaching that enlightenment is possible in this body may seem lofty, transformation is always possible. It all begins with the first step. We just need to decide what our pilgrimage will be.

Rev. Kosho Finch is head minister of Henjyoji Shingon Buddhist Temple in Portland, Oregon. He began his training at the Shingon temple in Sacramento, CA, and completed final ordination in Japan in 2006. He previously served as an assistant minister for the Shingon Mission of Hawaii. He completed the Shikoku pilgrimage in 2009, and hopes to undertake the pilgrimage again in the future.

Wisdom Facets From the Gem of Truth

Sri Ramakrishna

Holy Mother, Sri Sarada Devi

"It is Om To All"

"What is beyond speech and mind is born of the flesh, assuming various forms and engaging in various activities. From that one Om have sprung 'Om Siva,' 'Om Kali,' and 'Om Krishna.' Thus, God is both formless and endowed with form. He is many other things as well..."

(The Gospel of Sri Ramakrishna)

In the Subtle Body, Not the Physical Body

"An ardent devotee, following the Vedas, should hear something of the six centers. The mind of the aspiring yogi passes through these. Do you know what they are like? They are lotuses in the subtle body. The yogis see them. They are like the fruits and leaves of a wax tree."

(The Gospel of Sri Ramakrishna)

The Exemplar and the Exception

"Why are there such strict rules for a sannyasi? It is for the welfare of mankind as well as for his own good. A sannyasi may himself lead an unattached life, and may have controlled his passion, but he must renounce lust and greed to set an example to the world. On the other hand, it is not harmful for a householder who follows the path of knowledge to enjoy conjugal happiness with his wife now and then. He can satisfy the sexual impulse like any other natural desire."

(The Gospel of Sri Ramakrishna)

It is Mere Dust, Not Gold Dust

"Man loves his own wealth and riches, so he thinks that God loves them too. He thinks that God will be pleased if we glorify His riches. At the time of passing, he says, 'Please bless me that I can leave my wealth at the Lotus Feet of the Lord.' But such riches are riches only to him. What riches can one offer God? To Him, they are but dust and straw."

(The Gospel of Sri Ramakrishna)

Harmless Desires That Serve

"So long as the ego persists, desires will undoubtedly remain. But those desires will not hurt you if you let the Master be your protector. You must try to live in a spirit of service and self-surrender to Him."

(The Compassionate Mother)

Panchatapa Reflections

"When the preparations were made for the panchatapa ceremony, four fire pits were built in four corners of the square, each five cubits away from one another. Four big fires were set ablaze using dry cowdung cakes. Overhead was the blazing sun. After finishing my bath, I went there and saw the fires fully ablaze. A fear seized me, and I thought, how can I enter there and remain seated until sunset! Yogin Ma then said, 'Get in Mother, don't be afraid.' Then, with a silent prayer to the Master, I entered, and as I got in it felt like all the fires had lost their heat. Nonetheless, after doing this for five days, the body became like a charred log...."

(The Compassionate Mother)

From the Same Divine Root

"One day, the Master told me, 'I know who you and Lakshmi (Didi) are, but I shall not tell you. To repay my debt to you, I shall be born as a Baul and make you my companion.' I told him that Lakshmi said she would not come back here again even if she were chopped into shreds, like tobacco leaves. The Master laughed, and remarked, 'Where else can you be if I come again? You won't be able to survive separate from me. Our roots are twined together like the kalmi plant. Pull one stem and the whole clump comes forward.'"

(The Compassionate Mother)

Among Her Choicest Blessings

"I bless you on this holy day that you may attain liberation in this life. Birth and death are extremely painful. May you not suffer from them anymore."

(Sri Sarada Vijnanagita)

Wisdom Facets From the Gem of Truth

Painting by Swami Tadatmananda

Swami Vivekananda   Disciples & Devotees of Sri Ramakrishna

Try the Winds of Self-Effort

"Liberation, or samadhi, consists of doing away with the obstacles to the manifestation of Brahman. Otherwise, the Self is always shining forth like the sun. The cloud of your ignorance has only veiled it. Remove that cloud through spiritual disciplines and the sun will manifest its light."

(Talks with Swami Vivekananda)

A Question of More or Less...

"The more advanced a society or nation is in spirituality, the more is the society or nation civilized. No nation can be said to have become civilized only because it has succeeded in increasing the comforts of material life by bringing in lots of machinery and things of that sort. The present day civilization of the West is multiplying day by day only the wants and distresses of man. The ancient Indian civilization showed the way to spiritual advancement through lessening the material needs in men."

(Talks With Swami Vivekananda)

Rising Above Dualities

"What people in the West speak of as sin is just weakness; it is but another form of the egoistic idea of 'I am the body.' But when the mind gets steadfast in the Truth of 'I am the Self,' then one goes beyond merit and demerit, virtue and vice, etc."

(Talks With Swami Vivekananda)

The Real Shakti-Worshipper

"We want both men and women. We want thousands of them who will spread like wildfire from the Himalayas to Cape Comorin, from the North Pole to the South Pole, all over the world. The real Shakti-worshiper is he who knows that God is the Omnipresent force, and worships it in women."

(Swami Vivekananda Vijnanagita)

Salvation is in the Self, Not in Heaven

"Heaven should never be our ideal, not only because it is too small an ideal to strive for, but also because it holds no promise of further attainment. The constant pursuit of heavenly pleasures crowds out all spiritual effort. In this world we are to renounce enjoyments, and so in the next world as well."

(Swami Ramakrishnananda, Apostle of Ramakrishna)

Regarding Grief and Suffering

"Man has other things to do besides grieving. He has his worldly duties to attend to. Above everything else, he should progress towards the ideal of Life. Grieving does not profit a man. Life is not meant for suffering. We shall have to transcend birth, old age, and death, and realize God, the object of our supreme Love. Then alone there will come an end to sorrow. As Sri Krishna has said about the Atman,'...by attaining which all other attainments pale to insignificance, and being established in which one is not shaken by the heaviest of afflictions.'"

(Swami Sivananda, For Seekers of God)

The True Self is True Health

"All is to be done consciously. We must use direct concentration on the subconscious stratum of our being by the illumined consciousness of our true Self, or Atman. We do not have to deny sickness or affirm wholeness or exercise faith, but only have to rise into the superconscious state and fill our entire being with higher vibrations."

(Swami Abhedananda, Science of Psychic Phenomena)

A Brief Adoring Glance Certainly Cannot Hurt!

"To the man of wisdom the difference between the individual soul and the Paramahamsa has vanished, but he still continues his worship nevertheless. This is like the case of the husband and wife who are united in their hearts, yet the wife occasionally peeps at her lord through her veil."

(Swami Akhandananda, in Swami Akhandananda)

SCRIPTURAL SAYINGS
of the World's Religious Traditions

"May the partisans of all the doctrines in all countries around the world live in common fellowship for the highest good, here and hereafter. For all dharmic beings alike profess the aspiration that mastery is to be attained over oneself, and that purity of heart will be the result."

"Victory to the Essence of all Wisdom, to the Unmoving, to the Imperishable! Victory to the Eternal, to the essence of visible and invisible beings, who at the same time is the cause and the effect of the universe. I salute it reverently, this Supreme Deity, which is beyond the senses, which mind and speech cannot define, and which can be discerned only by the mind of the true sage."

"Whoever wishes to attain to the highest perfection of his being, and to the vision of the supreme good, must have a knowledge of himself and of the things that are all about him to the very core. This is only so that he can arrive at the supreme clarity. Therefore learn to know thyself, for that is far better for thee than to know all the powers of the creation."

"Happy is that one that findeth wisdom and getteth understanding. For its merchandise is far better than the merchandise of silver and gain of fine gold. She is more precious than rubies, and all the things that thou canst desire are not to be compared unto Her. Her ways are ways of contentment, and all Her paths are of Peace. She is the best tree of life to those who lay hold on Her, and verily happy are all that retaineth Her."

"I looked on High and I beheld in all the spaces That which is One; below, in all the foam of the waters, as well, That which is One; I looked into the heart, and perceived it was a sea, a space for worlds peopled with thousands of dreams: I saw in all the dreams That which is One."

"Something beyond the power of our discrimination existed before heaven and earth. How profound is its calm. How absolute its immateriality. It alone exists and does not change; It penetrates all and it does not perish. It may be regarded as the Mother of the Universe. For myself, I know not Its name, but to give it a name I would call It Tao. Even then, there is no suitable name for the eternal Tao..."

The Roots of Spiritual Suffering
& The Blessing of Immediate Awakening

This dharma talk was given in April of 2005, was transcribed by Roslyn Stark, and edited by Babaji Bob Kindler for inclusion into the Nectar of Nondual Truth journal via express permission of the Dharmata Foundation.

It's the last level of suffering in the world. This is not about suffering that we experience from poverty or social injustice; rather it is a spiritual suffering. This suffering can never be resolved by material and worldly well-being. We all have attempted to resolve this universal suffering by trying to pursue material and worldly riches, and yet we've failed; we failed every time anyone tried to resolve this suffering. Because this suffering really has nothing to do with what we have and don't have. It has nothing to do with whether we are poor, or being sick, or being unwanted by everybody else. This suffering has to do with the fact that we haven't realized our true essence.

The perfect resolution of suffering comes into being only in the moment when we realize our true essence. We can of course alter or modify the surface of this suffering simply by indulging sensual pleasures or cultivating worldly perfections, and yet we can never really cut to the very root of this suffering as long as we're living under the force of *avidya* or ignorance, thereby not recognizing our true essence. So in order to recognize our true essence, first we have to give up our hope and our expectations that the outer world or the ordinary life are going to bring us freedom and liberation; we have to give up that hope completely. We have to give up hope that the external conditions, the favorable circumstances, are going to bring about satisfaction to our inner hunger. We have to give up that hope. We have to give up that hope completely. If you do not give up that hope completely, then somehow or another we're only continuing to manage maintaining that very root of sorrow.

One Rinpoche explained it, that it would be like trying to ride a horse whose tail is tied to another horse's tail. You will get nowhere. No matter how strong and dynamic that horse might be, you will get nowhere. And no matter how enthusiastic, diligent, you might be, as long as you're still holding onto the hope that the outer world is going to bring about satisfaction, then there's no really true ground to reach that will help you transcend the source of sorrow.

There's a way that we hold onto this hope, these expectations, secretly, not letting ourself know that we're holding onto this hope secretly, you see? This is quite disquieting news. We withhold information from other people, but through self-inquiry we can realize that we have lots of information that's kept secret from ourselves too! It's quite shocking, actually, to discover that, through inquiry, through self-inquiry.

Sometimes you must think, "I've been doing everything I'm supposed to do. I've been practicing meditation, self-inquiry. I've been running to a lot of teachings. I even had a conscious moment of awakening, and yet my suffering, my confusion, is still continuing in my consciousness, what is going on?" You can sometimes easily get discouraged by not really finding any momentum of awakening in your life. The truth is, that you haven't really realized that you have been keeping all these *kleshas* away from yourself, you have been hiding these *kleshas* from yourself. And we are very good at hiding those *kleshas* from ourselves, those inner defilements. We succeed in hiding all this suffering information from ourselves through many lifetimes.

True Dharma Practice

So, the true *dharma* practice begins by disclosing all our secrets, all our tendencies, all our little games and self-deceptions to ourselves, and without any fear, any resistance. That's the only way we can really undertake the true journey of the *dharma*. If we can do that, which we should do sooner rather than later, then there is the possibility of ending the cycle of sorrow forever, eternally, if that's what we want.

I always say the word, "mercilessly;" this is one of my favorite words. Bear with me. I was writing a letter to someone, and somebody was helping with typing, and this person said, "Can I correct your English?" and I said, "Yes, go ahead." So I asked this person to correct my English, and this person said, with respect, "Can I suggest that you're using the words 'ruthless' and 'mercilessly' too much?" [much laughter] But actually, the truth is that this whole path is really all about being ruthless and merciless in the process of smashing and eradicating all your hopes, expectations, and illusions. That's *dharma* principle. You never can really change this principle for as long as you're on this journey. We never can change that *dharma* principle, whether we like it or not. Actually, we're going to like it once we start practicing in such a manner. Because it's only then that you can really bring about true, fresh, and raw awakening experience without delaying, without projecting enlightenment as an abstracted dimension, or as a reward that you can only achieve sometime in the future, or the next life.

Divine Discontent

So now what I'm really asking is that if you look into your consciousness now and then, you'll experience always this discontentment with your life. You're discontented. It's quite amazing to really realize that there is this ongoing sense of discontentment in each of us, in the minds of student, teachers, meditators, *yogis*, high *lamas*, taxi drivers, tax collectors as well, you see? There is this discontentment. And this discontentment comes along with insecurity, anger, confusion. And it's also quite amazing to realize how fragile our sense of existence is. Because our existence is the abode of lots of illusions, and those illusions are ready to collapse [Rinpoche snaps his fingers] at any moment. It's like a ramshackle house in India that collapses easily when there are earthquakes. It doesn't require a huge earthquake, either. Tiny earthquakes can collapse that funky house, you see. And that's how existence, life, is, actually.

Overweening Pride

And I imagine lots of people have a tremendous sense of pride. Of course, I'm not speaking just about other people; I also discovered there was a time in my life when I had a huge, enormous amount of pride. For no reason! [laughter] And that's what I see in a lot of people, too. And what pride is really about is a sense that I'm existing. More than that, I'm existing successfully in this universe. You see? My existence is glorious because I'm this and that, you see. I have all this certainty in my life, my social status, and especially the time I was part of what I call a *dharma* teenager. I was a *dharma* teenager. You know, once you recognize it totally, you become a *dharma* teenager. And they just can't kick you out from the monastery, no matter how mischievous or nasty you behave. [laughter] In that sense, I feel quite sympathetic with those self-righteous New Age teachers because they can get fired if they become like a *dharma* teenager. So notice I make jokes about that. Also, the *dharma* teenager has huge pride, too. We all have pride. And pride is quite convincing. Very powerful. It's very difficult to make that pride collapse because it gives you a sense of false satisfaction, and a real sense that life is under your control. You feel that both the known and the unknown are under your control. That's how illusory and misleading pride can be. How can we be in the control of unknown? How can we be in the control of reality? No one can be in the control of the unknown or the reality. So now you see, this pride comes with hope and expectation. So you will find that there is hope and expectation in our consciousness too. Look into that.

Actually, I was speaking about suffering just a few minutes ago. You'll find there's this ongoing, sort of, lurking suffering, what Buddha called *dukha*, or all-pervasive suffering. It's not the suffering of a life crisis or serious tragedy where you lose your body, or you lose your legs in a car accident, or you realize that you have a terminal illness, or you realize that you're about to lose everything that you have earned. That's life crisis. Suffering is different from a life crisis or tragedy. That's why Buddha called it *dukha*. It's quite difficult to translate that term *dukha* into English because we already have a preconceived notion of suffering. People usually think automatically of suffering as either a physical or internal psychological crisis, like tragedy. We don't have any idea that there is this ongoing existential suffering, and that it pretty much is dominating our life, day and night, twenty-four hours a day. Until there is a true moment of awakening we don't know that. I think that's why illusion is so successful in terms of seducing and deceiving everybody not to give out their highest aspiration and love to the truth. So what we did, we gave out love and aspiration to the illusion, to the *maya*, rather than to the truth or to the *Dharmakaya*. Because illusion is quite successful in deceiving us.

But that suffering has to be acknowledged, has to be brought up under the light of awareness. And when that happens, then it is then that it can really cause us authentic genuine aspiration

> "We never can change that dharma principle, whether we like it or not. Actually, we're going to like it once we start practicing in such a manner. Because it's only then that you can really bring about true, fresh, and raw awakening experience without delaying, without projecting enlightenment as an abstracted dimension, or as a reward that you can only achieve sometime in the future, or the next life."

towards awakening. Not when we are just going back and forth, running around and doing spiritual window-shopping. Or simply trying to use all sort of spiritual practice, doing *dharma* to just create a further illusion, create a further defense between yourself and the realization of truth. Because that happens quite a lot. *Dharma* can be used to create further illusion. That's why one great Tibetan master said, if you don't practice *dharma* as *dharma*, *dharma* can be a source of *samsara*. Because there's a superficial fascination and curiosity about *buddha-dharma* or *Buddhism*, and that kind of superficial fascination can be the very motive why they are engaging in the *dharma* practice in the first place, without having that genuine wholehearted aspiration to the great awakening.

The Auspicious Timing of Spiritual Awakening

I believe that once you have that wholehearted aspiration towards the path and towards awakening, the liberation is going to come to you very soon. It always comes that way; it never delays for long. Liberation never says, "Sorry, I had a car accident," or "I had a flat tire and that's why I was late." It never says that. We're the ones who are saying that, right? When we try to come to puja teachings it is like, oops, oh, I had a flat tire, or I didn't know that daylight savings time was operating, and that's why I missed the puja. You see? [laughter] "I realized that I had another scheduled commitment, and that's why I couldn't show up to the teachings or to meditation." You see? But liberation never says that. It always comes right now.

So, liberation is always waiting anxiously to be in union with you. Just think of that, there is this liberation, there is this awakening always wanting to be with you. You see, sometimes you feel when you are in a pure state of consciousness, you feel that you have so much love, you have so much knowing, you have so much devotion, and wanting to be in union with awakening, with Buddha or with truth. And this imminent liberation, awakening, has that one longing to be one with you. The difference is, that we have that longing now and then, right? Once a week? Whereas liberation is always longing to be with us [snaps his fingers] each and every moment. And that's why there's not really a reason, there's not any excuses why you cannot be awakened – eternally, completely, in this life. If you can cultivate that genuine aspiration toward the path and the great awakening, that's all you need to do.

But how can we invoke that powerful passionate and genuine aspiration towards the *dharma* and towards awakening above everything else? The only way we can initiate that aspiration is through realizing that something's not working in our life, but everything seems to be working in life. And that is why we're still bonded to suffering due to our ordinary unawakened mind telling us that everything's going well. Illusion pretends to be your only refuge. You see, that's how ordinary mind cannot be the refuge you have. There's always the place that you have to determine whether you're going to be successful or fail or lose; almost this Christian version of hell and heaven, you know. This is the only chance you have. This illusion is the last refuge, so you have got to be successful. This illusion, in this ordinary world, if you fail in this world, then you failed eternally...that's what your unawakened mind is telling you. And that you have to be somebody that everyone knows, and that's why you have to have more than what you have. And that's why you always hear that what you are is not enough and what you have is not complete.

And once you cultivate that wholehearted, passionate aspiration toward awakening, then that's where liberation knocks on your door, and beckons you. Liberation wants to enter into your life, voluntarily. You don't have to exert so much effort to be awakened. Liberation comes to you always, because your heart is open now, and all the boundaries between you and the reality have been collapsed completely. Liberation always comes to you because liberation is also always longing to be in union with you, each and every moment. Therefore, you arrive at that place in your journey where your relationship and your approach to the *dharma* is no longer a mere idea and no longer a doubtful speculation, no longer an imagination or an ego-show, then it has arrived at that pure devotion. When that happens, liberation comes to you very easy. I'm sure that happens then, as I was just saying earlier, and no matter how much we exert, how much effort we put there in order to pursue liberation or enlightenment, we'll never be able to completely arrive there otherwise. We'll never be able to completely bring about the great awakening of Consciousness, because we really haven't arrived at the essence of *dharma*. We haven't cut through the very force, the *karmic* force, the egoist force that is binding us to the illusion, to the sorrow.

Inner Work, Right Now!

So now I'm going to ask everybody to just do a brief self-inquiry. Look into your mind, into your heart right now, and be honest with yourself as much as you can. Let yourself go to the place in your consciousness where there is hope and there is expectation. Hope to be enlightened. Hope to be awakened, even. Hope to be successful. Hope that everyone is going to love you. Hope that you can get what you want. And realize that hope and expectation, so deeply seated and entrenched in our mind and heart, even as an image has been carved on stone, on a diamond, even. If we cannot let go of that hope, then somehow or another our life is going to collapse. Everything is going to be ruined. You see? We falsely feel that we have to hold onto that hope to ensure our life and our existence.

Our practice is always, mercilessly again, allowing ourself into our own consciousness, in that place in our consciousness that we

> "Liberation never says, 'Sorry, I had a car accident,' or 'I had a flat tire and that's why I was late.' We're the ones who are saying that, right? When we try to come to puja teachings it is like, oops, 'oh, I had a flat tire,' or 'I didn't know that daylight savings time was operating, and that's why I missed the puja.' You see? [laughter] 'I realized that I had another scheduled commitment, and that's why I couldn't show up to the teachings or to meditation.' You see? But liberation never says that. It always comes right now."

haven't really charted and mapped, then go there and to find this demon – the demon of hope, the demon of expectation, the demon of imagination – and bring all of them under the light of recognition and awareness. And just right there, right there, you let go of all of them. Do so no matter how much propaganda, terrifying propaganda, the ego may deliver you. Ego will tell you, you cannot do that, don't you realize you are brainwashed right now, don't you realize that you are cheating on yourself, don't you realize that you are going to lose your sense of security? Don't do that. Your ego is telling you that you just can't do that, you see? Or, your ego may be telling you right now, "well, I understand that what you're doing is kind of spiritual, but there is something better than this." [laughter] Right? It tells you, even when you follow this recipe of spiritual practice, it's supposed to be very more powerful than what you're doing right now. Ego is quite smart. Ego might tell you, well, what's the name of your practice? You don't have any name, right? Why should you be tied to a practice?

But you have to let go everything, all the demons of hope, and expectation, and fear. Right there. That's all you need to do. Because there's nothing to do and there's nothing to know, there's nothing to realize. You just have to let go all these demons of hope and fear, right? And not hold onto them any longer. And no longer will you identify them as the source of your existence. And when you can do that, then, right there, the liberation will come to you. Because there's no real, solid boundary that's keeping you and the truth apart from each other. You only imagine that mental demons of hope and fear are setting a boundary between you and reality. When they are completely collapsed, then you realize that you have been always awakened, you have been always *buddha* nature from the beginning.

After The Demon's Demise

The amazing thing about this practice is that there's no process. There's no process at all! All you need to do is you just pause now and then and you vow, you pledge, to do this practice, the practice that is whatever you like to call it. You can call it *Mahamudra*, or *Samatha*, or *Dzogchen*, or awareness meditation; you can call it whatever you like, this simple meditation. But this meditation does not have any process. So then you just pause and then you just practice the way I described right now. And do not make this practice more complicated than it is, because it is truly simple. And every time you go through this practice, this meditation that I described, you will always realize awareness, you will always realize the pure essence of the *Dharmata*, right there. You will like that. It's absolutely granted that you are always going to be awake if you just do this simple practice without adding anything to it, and without taking away anything from it.

So now, just think about it. Do you really want to drink the water, or do you just want to drink water. You see? If you really want to drink water, just water, then you're not supposed to add anything to the water. You're not supposed to add anything, like sugar, or wine, or milk, or ambrosia. Somebody may tell you, well, you want to drink only water but it would be nice if you add ambrosia into the water. It sounds very convincing, right? Enticing. And you might want to add ambrosia into the water, which is good, but the problem is that you really are not drinking the real water, the authentic water. So you don't want to add anything to the water. We really want to drink just water. And similarly, you cannot take anything away from the water either. So this practice is like that, drinking the pure water, just water. Without adding anything, without subtracting anything. So, just practice exactly in the same manner that I described a few minutes ago. And there's this guarantee, this absolute guarantee, that each of us is going to experience that ultimate awakening right there, and on the spot.

I'm going to offer a prayer: May you all undertake the path of wisdom and ultimate bliss, and may all of you discover the highest liberation in this life through the path of the *dakini*. May you also bring forward your innate qualities such as love, wisdom, and compassion, towards the countless beings in your life. May you not only have the ability to transform yourself, but to transform everyone, and transform this entire world.

Thank you, everybody.

ANAM THUBTEN grew up in Tibet and at an early age began to practice in the Nyingma tradition of Tibetan Buddhism. He is the founder and spiritual advisor of the Dharmata Foundation, and he teaches widely in the United States and internationally.

My Experience in Samsara
A Spontaneous Song by Milarepa
(Sung for a woman who asked him about his life)

At first, my experience in samsara
seemed most pleasant and delightful.
Later, I learned its lessons.
In the end I found it a demonic prison.
These are my thoughts and feelings about samsara.
So I made up my mind to renounce it.

At first, samsara appears to be one's friend.
She is like a smiling angel.
Later, she turns into an exasperated woman.
In the end, a demoness is she.
These are my thoughts about samsaric companions.
So I decided to renounce samsaric friendship.

At first, samsara seems to be a sweet boy
who smiles; a babe of heaven.
Later, he makes trouble with the neighbors.
In the end, he is my creditor and foe.
These are my thoughts about children in samsara.
So I renounced the sons and nephews of samsara.

At first, the money of samsara pretends to be
the wish-fulfilling gem that can promise everything.
Later, one cannot do without it.
In the end, one becomes a penniless beggar.
These are my thoughts about samsaric money.
So I renounced wealth used for samsaric purposes.

When I think of these experiences of samsara,
I cannot help but practice the dharma —
the teachings of enlightenment.
When I think of the dharma,
the way to enlightenment,
I cannot help but offer it to others.

When samsaric death approaches,
I shall have no regrets.

Babaji Bob Kindler

GOING BEYOND THE INTELLECTUAL FRAME OF REFERENCE
Where Jivanmukti-hood Awaits

Transcendent of the earth-bound body, the matter-oriented mind, and the heaven-aspiring senses, there is the realm of Intelligence that is known to the seers of Consciousness as The Cosmic Mind, The Word, Mother Wisdom, Living Intelligence, and more. It has been called the *Buddhi* as well, a title which Lord Buddha donned upon himself. That special Intelligence exists both prior to and beyond its container (the intellect). It is wisely sequestered out and away from all that attempts to limit it by the seers, just as the mind is astutely discerned as being different from the brain by deeper Indian thinkers. The phrase, Limitless Intelligence, could also be used to describe it.

Beyond the physical, the etheric, and the celestial, then, yet falling short of this lofty aforementioned level of conscious Intelligence, is a cross-section of mind imbued with conventional considerations, conjectural thought, willful conceptualization, and unbridled imagination. This is the intellect proper, which cuts for itself borders of knowing and not-knowing, seeing and not-seeing, projecting and forgetting, fashioning and dissolving, all in conjunction with the finite universe consisting of matter alone. Though thinking itself quite grand (when it is in conjunction with the arrogant, unripe ego), it is actually the king of delimitation. It is here, in this realm of space and time imagined to be real, that the discoveries of modern man, particularly of the Western mind, get restricted to. All of life, as it is known to the human being, becomes posited there, and firmly pinioned there as well. All that is anterior to it, similar to the sense of existence that precedes birth, and all that lies beyond it, such as the metaphysical, the interior realms, and the source of its own awareness, remains unknown to it — to its "intellectual frame of reference."

The All-Penetrating Fire of Yogic Intelligence

Intelligence itself is like fire; it can burn through all substances, thick or thin, when unleashed and applied to them. It is therefore strange indeed that a tool with such potential has been allowed to rust and become dull, thus rendered inadequate to the higher task of informing the human mind of what lies beyond it. The Indian seers say that to hone the intellect (*buddhi*) using the sharpening tools of higher wisdom (*jnanam*), meditation on Reality (*dhyanam*), and realization of the nondual nature of Existence (*advaitayam*), will make it equal to the task of erasing the line of demarcation between the intellect and its subtler counterpart, the Cosmic Mind (*Mahat*), thereby allowing it to transcend the idea of relativity overall.

And it is here that one would begin to see the marked difference between an intellectual or a genius, and a realized seer or luminary; in other words, between a Western scientist focused upon matter and its potentially destructive power, and an Eastern *rishi/yogi* experiencing the bliss of pure, conscious Awareness. The latter brings peace and *karma*-free prosperity into the world of mortals, while the latter brings an alluring power (occult *siddhi*) that risks acts of violent domination and destructive urges married to a life of mere pleasure-seeking as the goal of human existence. This dim and dangerous prospect, courted and supported by so many Western physicists, psychologists, and philosophers, is rejected by the *dharmic* (righteous) soul who is, by the way, utilizing the power of living Intelligence for its designated and predestined purpose. It will duly dis-integrate all that the lower mind in *Maya* attempts to integrate. The darkness-born ignorance of ages coveted by low-minded thinkers (*asuras*) will then be turned to ashes, which the Great Renouncers will then smear across their brow and body with ecstatic smiles. As Swami Aseshanandaji Maharaj said, in current times: "*The concentrated mind is like the rays of the sun when you catch them under a lens; that power is to be conserved, for it brings inner light to the soul. Ironically, scientific investigation, which brings wonderful discoveries to society, owes its success to this selfsame power of concentrated mind. In its case, however, it became focused on the mutable object. Fine. Now simply focus it back upon the Eternal Subject.*"

Great luminaries of India have been aware of the "Fire of Living Intelligence" for eons. Seeing the restricted arena of Western intellectual thinking when he arrived in England and America in the late 1800's, Swami Vivekananda intimated this lofty solution by stating, "*Sitting up on the snow peaks of the Himalayas, I repeat from the Upanisads: 'He has neither disease, nor decay, nor death, for, verily, he has obtained a body full of the fire of Yoga.'*" In the mid 1900's, Swami Aseshanandaji, spoke further on the important subject, saying: "*If a Western scientist would say that matter is akin to consciousness via thought, then he might transcend the scientific plane; he would become a mystic. But here is not just mysticism, it is realization, nirvikalpa samadhi. That is why Swami Brahmananda declares in the Eternal Companion, 'Show me the line of demarcation where matter ends and spirit begins.'*"

Cosmic, Collective, and Common Compartmentalization

The initial compartmentalization that man suffers is one of cosmic design, wherein the causal seeds of nature (unmanifested *Prakriti*) get watered by a Great Power, like Lord *Brahma* and the *Trimurti*. In the hands of the cosmic subterfuge of *Maya*, the second form of delimitation that mankind falls into is one of intellectualization; this is threefold: there is the "first compound of Consciousness" called conscious Intelligence; then there is the sheath of intellect, or buddhi; and third, the limited knowledge that infills the sheath. Falling lower than these three realms of thought and thinking is the solidification of thought into objects, now become the realm of matter.

Unbeknownst to many, objects are just thought turned solid, or made concretized (in the waking state). Those who occupy the "matter only" realm of delimitation imagine the object to be real,

> "Metaphorically speaking, jumping into three pools of saltwater, each larger than the last, but walking away from the ocean that formed all three without immersing there, would describe an intellectual's failure to penetrate his own self-actuated frame of reference with regards to the mind and intellect."

and covet it for power and pleasure. Those who move to inhabit the "intellect only" realm of delimitation plunge into the internal activities of thinking and conceptualizing as the highest occupation. Awakened souls, however, free of all types of imagination (*sankalpa*), go beyond the sheath of the intellectual frame of reference and soon become *jivanmuktas*, living-liberated beings. Nevertheless, it is all "Living Intelligence" — pure, conscious, and imbued with inherent Sentiency — that is being delimited.

The source of Intelligence is Consciousness, what India has always thought of as God, or *Brahman*. That cannot not be restricted to any space, within or without. As Swami Aseshanandaji stated, again: "*Recently, quantum physicists are speaking of the scientist being both a participant and an observer. Some scientists are calling consciousness singular, never dual or plural. When they speak like that they are talking like illumined souls, but unfortunately they do not follow the method of transcending the intellect and finally reaching Nirvikalpa Samadhi.*" So, importantly, recognizing a vibrationally hushed echelon, finer by degree than one's own wisdom, depends upon directly experiencing Consciousness rather than only utilizing its mediums. Metaphorically speaking, jumping into three pools of saltwater, each larger than the last, but walking away from the ocean that formed all three without immersing there, would describe an intellectual's failure to penetrate his own self-actuated frame of reference with regards to the mind and intellect. Beyond intellectual knowledge, then, is spiritual experience, called *anubhava*. The difference between the two is likened by the seers as looking on a map to find the location of one's destination as opposed to actually traveling there and experiencing it for oneself.

Dangers of the Intellectual Frame of Reference

The need for piercing through the subtle barrier of the intellect is not so subtle. Mankind, in the present age, has remained poised on the brink of the possibilities of inward exploration of Consciousness for some time, but is ever-tending, opting, to go outwards instead. The inner discoveries are close to the Source, i.e., his own nature/Ultimate Reality. What is external is all restless, desire-laden expression (as in the busy life and world), and empty projection (as in a substanceless dream). Therefore, intelligence co-opted by the intellect for use by the intellectual has produced two categories of suffering: weapons for mass destruction and domination; and objects for pleasure and personification. But the foremost qualities of refined Intelligence are amelioration and illumination, the former to benefit life on earth, and the latter to help transcend dependence upon matter and realize Spirit, or Consciousness. As Sri Krishna has stated in the Bhagavad Gita, Knowledge that does not mature into Truth becomes dangerous. This predicament is likened to waiting around near a lighted stick of dynamite to see if the wick works.

In arenas other than scientific, intelligence that is trapped within the unawakened human mind undergoes the risk of being taken over by the human ego. The assumed possession of knowledge leads to premature conclusions in life and in nature, which in turn results in the growth of a false sense of agency. This latter insinuation gives rise to uninformed actions and incomplete works. Completely opposite of this is that indescribably buoyant feeling that proceeds from giving away all possession of one's personal thoughts and vaunted inventions to a higher power, one that is not only akin to the "Fire of Living Intelligence," (see chart on facing page) but is the purveyor of it as well. Swami Aseshanandaji pointed to this unique Presence in one of his discourses, saying: "*Western man accepts objective experience only. However, if you look, in meditation, behind the phenomenal universe, you will see the Infinite Spirit, The Divine Mother, the Eternal Subject.*"

The oversight of failing to perceive the inherent Power (*Shakti*) in everything is certainly one of the obvious dangers in manning and holding onto the intellectual frame of reference, as Western savants have been naively doing for far too long now. It is actually demeaning to the intelligence vested in mankind's precious awareness to relegate such wondrous potential to occupations such as courting and storing up physical power, only to betray his own intelligence in the interim by letting destruction loose upon members of his own species.

Burning Conclusion

Thinking of the nearness and dearness of his or her own family, and the care with which his precious mother brought him up, mankind should look to the Mother of the Universe, whose perfect Intelligence, springing from nondual Awareness, reveals all levels of knowledge, plus higher Wisdom, to the mind and entire being. Even as vast as the physical space one gazes into nightly certainly is, deeper by far is Her abiding Presence, graced eternally by Her all-pervasive, Living Intelligence.

Babaji Bob Kindler, initiated disciple of Swami Aseshanandaji Maharaj, is the Spiritual Director of the SRV Associations with its two main centers in Hawaii and Oregon. A teacher of religion and spirituality and a prolific author, his books include The Avadhut, Twenty-Four Aspects of Mother Kali, Ten Divine Articles of Sri Durga, Swami Vivekananda Vijnanagita, Sri Sarada Vijnanagita, An Extensive Anthology of Sri Ramakrishna's Stories, A Quintessential Yoga Vasishtha, Reclaiming Kundalini Yoga, Cosmic Quintuplications, Jnana Matra, Manasana, Footfalls of the Indian Rishis, and others. Founder and Artistic Director of Jai Ma Music, he is also an accomplished musician, recording artist, and composer, who has produced over twenty-five albums of instrumental and devotional music.

 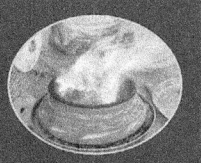

The Flame, Fuel, & Heat of the Fire of Yoga

"He has neither disease, nor decay, nor death, for, verily, he has obtained a body full of the Fire of Yoga." Swami Vivekananda

Heat
Grace, Inspiration, Wisdom Transmission

1. Dispels limitations by the power inherent in words of Wisdom
2. Radiates as the vibration of focused Awareness
3. Heals the body, purifies prana, clarifies mind, and hones the intellect
4. Conducts Consciousness into its primal Spiritual Centers

"I know that sacred fire which leads to heaven and beyond. Listen. That fire which is the means of attaining the infinite worlds, and is also their foundation — it is hidden in the sacred place of the heart."
Katha Upanisad

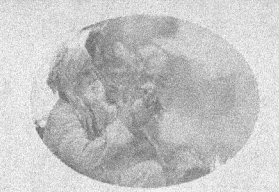

"The fire of Yoga burns the cage of sin that is around a man. Knowledge becomes purified and Nirvana is directly obtained. From Yoga comes Knowledge; Knowledge again helps the Yogi. He, who combines in himself both Yoga and Knowledge, with him the Lord is highly pleased."
Swami Vivekananda

The All-Consuming Fire of Yoga

Flame
Rishi, Preceptor, Guru, Acharya

1. Acts as an Exemplar for Enlightenment on earth, in the body
2. Shows the spiritual aspirant the Path leading to Freedom
3. Sheds light upon the Scriptures to reveal their Timeless Message
4. Clarifies the fact that Brahman is the Only Reality

Fuel
Knowledge, Maya, Ignorance, Delusion

1. Devours delusion and ignorance like fire consumes wood
2. Exposes Maya like a forest fire lights up nocturnal skies
3. Turns Aparavidya into dry kindling, blazing the path to Paravidya
4. Reduces even Wisdom to ashes, to be blown away by the winds of Nondual Realization

"Like the fetus well preserved by the pregnant mother, the omniscient fire hidden in fire sticks is worshipped day after day by awakened souls and wise sacrificers. Make of your lower self one stick, and rub it against the stick of the higher Self to produce illumination." Katha Upanisad

◆ DEACON PETER SOLAN

CHRIST:
The Teacher in My Life

FROM THE MOMENT WE ARE BORN we are surrounded by people who influence our lives. Whether conscious or unconscious of this fact, we are all students and teachers to one another at various points and levels. Accepting this principle, the paradigm shifts to our relationship as student or teacher with each other, and our understanding of that relationship. Before we can understand, appreciate, and integrate the teachings into our lives, I believe we must first understand and accept the relationship of self to Self. Thus, at this point in my life, I must ask myself to honestly evaluate the state of body and Spirit. This means I must accept the fact that I live in duality, in worldly consciousness or "illusions" that are very real to this plane of existence, yet subject to spiritual Consciousness, or God-consciousness. Without the realization of spiritual Consciousness, both teaching and learning become a moot point. If I believe that I live and act in worldly consciousness, my learning and teaching will be merely one dimensional, centered only in self-gratification. With the realization of spiritual Consciousness, I live in full communion with the Supreme Being.

In this world we find ourselves on a journey, always coming from some place, going to another. Learning becomes that "ah ha" moment of enlightenment between these two points that moves us to accept or reject the path we find ourselves on. To nurture that "ah ha" moment forward is to change. In the design of free will, the choice becomes ours to make. As students, therefore, we must with great care and discernment choose our teachers wisely because our destination is often the fruit of what path we choose.

When we are born, we are introduced into a culture of truths, philosophy, and faith. These principles begin to mold us as individuals as we continue our journey. This process in itself is an experience of faith to some degree, for often we know no better. At some point, however, we find ourselves assimilated into the Reality. In many cultures, that body and spirit coexist is the normal or standard conception. Our true journey begins when something clicks within, and the whispers of duality let go of our conscious mind and we choose to move in another direction. So begins the quest.

Christian Monotheism

Being raised a Christian, I have come to accept and believe in a monotheistic God. Yet, within this oneness lives a great mystery that faith fathers, philosophers and theologians have spoken and written about since the time of Abraham. As Christians, we believe this mystery did not begin with Abraham, for Truth as we know it is ever unchanging. Thus our prayer: "Glory be to the Father, to the Son and to the Holy Spirit, one God who always was, is now, and will be without end. Amen"

Within this trinity lives my Teacher, known to the world as the Christ, the Son of God made manifest as Rabboni – the "teacher" who reveals Himself to the world. Simply put, He comes to teach, reveal, and exemplify the Reality we are called to live as true children of God. Be the child He created you to be! It should be so simple! Simple it is, but enter said duality, and this simplicity of being becomes a complex struggle between "my will" and "Thy will." This again raises the age old question, "Who is God?" Who is the creator and who is the created?"

If we examine Christian Scripture, in the book of Genesis, all was well. There was no sin, no sickness, no death until Adam and Eve ate from the tree of the knowledge of Good and Evil. With that act, the fruit of that decision, "the desire to be God," brought about a breach in creation. Not that by design God created the breach, but rather the fruit was the result of accepting, acting out, and enforcing "my will" rather than "Thy Will."

If we searched the paths of our lives, I believe we could all come up with a credo that encapsulates who we are. The credo of my teacher Christ can be reduced to one phrase: "Thy will be done." We need only read the gospels of Matthew, Mark, Luke and John to see the pattern of the Rabboni emerge. Not a single act, decision, or manifestation was stated or performed without entering into communion, "relationship," with God, the Father. This "relationship" sheds light when the struggle of dual opposites come into play, and when important choices need to be made. In turn, these acts displayed God, the Father, as having compassion and power through unconditional love and understanding, further overseeing that all beings and their lives be drawn into "relationship" with all of creation and the Self. This is an important concept in understanding Christianity.

Christ the Exemplar

Christ teaches through words, but more often through His actions, and then it is not the act but rather the foundation of relationship that is taught. For what is taught by Christ, what is lived by Christ is nothing less than the will of God. And in living in the will of God total fulfillment is eventually realized as was lived before the great breach.

We believe Christ came to show us the way back to God. Up until His incarnation, and ever since the fall of mankind through Adam and Eve, a breach developed that needed to be bridged so that Creator and created could once again celebrate total unity. Through time, most of mankind chose the credo of "my will" again and again. In doing so, humanity availed and restricted itself to the gains of worldly consciousness and suffered the effects such as natural disasters, slavery, alienation, sickness and perception of eternal death. These are the bitter fruits of living an unenlightened existence based upon duality.

As creation unfolded throughout time, the light of Truth was whispered to the kings and prophets of their day, and to the Jewish people. Within these whispers was the flicker of hope that humanity would be graced with the anointed of God. The anointed would teach them Godly ways and bring them back to the covenant with Him. Through the anointed one, all humanity would be lead back across this breach, this wide chasm, and once again find unity with God. The Gospel of John thus begins:

*"In the beginning was the word,
and the word was with God,
and the word was God.
He was in the beginning with God.
All things came to be through Him,
And without Him nothing came to be.
What came to be through Him was life.
And this life was the light of the human race.
This light shone in the darkness.
Darkness has not overcome it."*

On a personal level, then, I was inculturated into the light. As an adult, and looking back on my journey, it becomes painfully clear that many times I chose to live in worldly consciousness and thus suffered because of my unenlightened ways. Yet that inner light always whispered to my conscious Self, for even though I have the power to turn from the flame, I have not the power to extinguish it. God desires to be in relationship so much with us that even in our darkest hour, His flame, His presence remains vigilant and leads us from darkness back to safety.

As a student, through my own experience I can honestly say that I live for my teacher. Yes, the lessons have been many, some lessons have been hard, but no lesson has ever brought me to the darkness; rather only to the light. Anytime this journey pauses and I reflect upon it, it becomes crystal clear that in every case, every road traveled has led me closer to God, and has always been through "Thy will, not my will."

In reading the Gospels of Jesus, the problems of fear, hate, alienation, sin, illness, poverty and death crescendo to form some of the greatest teachings for a student. The relative realities are balanced by the heavenly truths of God. So many teachings, so little time in my life to appreciate them all. So I attempt to come up with an example to clarify and shed light upon my own words – to try to pinpoint who Christ the Teacher is for me. But, alas, I am at a loss for words, for merely speaking about Truth always falls short. Yet, my Teacher calls me with powerful words, real words, and His voice is a call to true action.

Jesus came into the world at a time when humanity had been reduced to observing crystallized laws. Through these laws only, one experienced a relationship with God. Often the law became so severe that religious leaders wound up dictating to God and humanity. But Jesus speaks for Himself and knows what is required to have a relationship with God.

In my own life, the one thing that haunts me is that great teaching of the credo of Jesus, "Thy will, not my will." It is so simple yet so complex, for His will encompasses every singular act I am called to do, and so defines my destiny if I am truly a child of God. In all great religions, beings are called to emulate the great masters and teachers. Christ came to reclaim the dignity of fallen humanity by living out the loving reality of God.

Christ used words, parables and acts to show us how to live and love in God's light. Through His own testament, like the seamless garment we read about at His Calvary, it becomes my cloak and the cloak of all Christians, for I cannot compromise a single act or a single word and still hold His teachings intact. My Teacher has taught me by the example of His own life. I cannot simply speak of God's love, peace, and forgiveness without living it in every breath I take, even if it is to be my final breath.

As a Christian, I struggle daily with those great words of Christ – "Thy will, not my will." For every time I emerge from a new lesson, the Teacher is all around me, calling me into a greater understanding. For, once I have entered into relationship with Him, I become Him. I am His agent, I am His eyes, His ears, His hands, His presence in this life of seeming duality. Christ has therefore taught me to shed the veil of illusion called "my will" and seek only the greater good called "Thy will." "His will" is why I was ordained. I have been blessed with the grace to see. I am a blessed student, for my Teacher has shown me the way. I realize, then, that I am part of a bigger picture. I have my own place within creation. We are called to be the Christ for each other, called to be both student and teacher. This is part of the cycle of creation and the truth of existence. The cycles are ever in flux, always changing. My Teacher has stated that we all have a part in that change – the change that takes place for the further journey which lies before us.

I would like to end with a prayer adapted from Sister Ruth Marlene Fox OSB, for it speaks of the specific actions and reflects the words that Christ the Teacher has taught me:

"May God bless you with discontent at easy answer, half-truths, superficial relationships, so that you will live from deep within your heart. May God bless you with anger at injustice, oppression, abuse and exploitation of people, so that you will work for justice, equality, and peace. May God bless you with tears to shed for those who suffer from pain, rejection, starvation and war, so that you will reach out your hand to comfort them and to change their pain into joy.

May God bless you with the foolishness to think you can make a difference in this world, so that you will do the things which others tell you cannot be done. And may God the Holy Spirit bless you with happiness, inner peace, laughter, and faithful friends, as you continue on your journeys as members of the Body of Christ."

Deacon Peter A. Solan, O.C.D.S., Order of Carmelites Discalsed Secular, has his B.A.in philosophy and religious education from Merrimack College, Boston. Ordained deacon in 1995, he was then assigned to St. Peter's Catholic Church, Pacifica, CA. and to St. Mary of the Assumption's Cathedral, San Francisco, CA.

◆ BABAJI BOB KINDLER

GODBLOGS
Brahman-Bytes

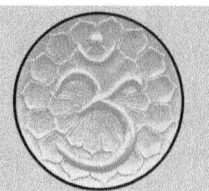

Hundreds of "Godblogs," also titled "Brahman-bytes," appear on SRV Association's website, ASR (Ashram of the Subtle Realms) most every weekday, and are discussed on line with Babaji every Saturday with the SRV sangha, friends, participants, and visitors as well. Become a member at: community@srvwisdom.org

The Overcast Sky of the World
How to Escape a Dark Room

The Light of Spirituality is much different than the light of the sun. Similarly, the darkness of a damp cave is dissimilar to the deep, luminous blackness of nocturnal skies. Additionally, the activities of everyday life in the world differ from the static peace of rapt meditation. Such contrasts are to be noted, and specific lessons are to be taken from them. An *Avatar*, like Sri Ramakrishna, can shed light upon these distinctions, empowering the soul to awaken and reach the goal of human existence. Examples of this are to be found in many of his words: *"There is mostly suffering in the world. The world is like an overcast sky that steadily pours down rain: the face of the sun is seldom seen. On account of the cloud of lust and greed beings cannot see the sun. Coming out of the dark room of the world one encounters the sun of Wisdom. The sun's rays that fall on a lens burn away all objects. So come out of the room and use the lens."*

The effects of deeds done in previous lifetimes follow the reincarnated being into embodiment. In so many cases, those actions were ill-considered, poorly enacted, or unconsciously engaged in. This makes them much like a boomerang which verily returns to its owner when cast away. As the present life ensues, the return of this amassed *karma* (*prarabdha*) can easily overshadow life, casting the gloom of death, fear, doubt, and darkness over the soul. In this way the worldly personage wanders about to the four corners of the earth for the sake of happiness. He does not find it, and only becomes tired and weary.

If dispassion comes to living beings after some experience in the world, they might attain *jnanam*. The *jnani* can live in the world and see the Light of God illuminating it. In the Gospel, Sri Ramakrishna describes the *jnani* well: *"The jnani discovers the light of wisdom that illumines the world. The perfect jnani sometimes seems like a perfect fool. He scarcely discriminates anymore between good and bad, holy and unholy. Perhaps he does not use the mantra anymore. If he offers flowers, he offers them everywhere, not just to one image. Such a soul lives in the world as if in a glass house, seeing both inside and outside clearly. All others live in mud huts with no windows."* Therefore, may every habitation we lodge in within the realms of name and form have clear windows to see out of and open doorways to move ever inwards through.

AUM Shanti, Shanti, Shanti. Om Peace, Peace, Peace!

The Age of Darkness?
Why Send in the Clowns? Send in the Seers!

The saying which states, "It is always darkest before the dawn," is never seen to be more true then when it is cast in the light of the spiritual path. For those who have set resolute feet upon the Eternal Path, darkness becomes their friend, radiant with the sheen of hidden Awareness. Out of such pitch, black Presence, termed Kali, emerges the *Avatar* and His subtle minions. The luminous space around Her becomes Her clothing, and they call Her *Digambari*. In the presence of Her children, worldly poison turns to Nectar, and they drink it in, contentedly. As the Holy Mother has stated: *"That you have been born in the Kali Yuga, this particular age, is a great blessing. For, this is the time you can actually see His divine sport. One can easily see this play of Consciousness if one looks upon it with faith and devotion."*

The world, today, can be likened to an old, weathered, creaking, sailing schooner, weighted down with tons of old, unwanted *karmic* cargo, its leaking hold filled with the sloshing bilge water of countless unwise actions. Its topsail of voyaging victory is gone, its mainsail of

forward progress is torn and tattered, and the captain is often seen missing from his post at the wheel on the bridge due to his inebriation from the grog of countless insipid pleasures. His crew is benighted humanity, beset with all the cares and worries that usually frighten mortal beings lost at sea. The ship's compass has long since become waterlogged by the numerous waves of desire that are constantly washing up and over the lumbering craft's slippery decks. This ship of fools wanders aimlessly over the vast ocean expanses of meaninglessness, much like a physical world that spins through heartless, vacuous space.

And yet, the Divine Mother's children, embodied in this very world, sing, *"O Mother Supreme in Human Form, granter of boons and of bliss, distress of our souls removest thou, and givest us contentment and peace."* Sri Sarada Devi, the Holy Mother Herself, was seen by the Avatar of this age of darkness as Mother Kali manifest on earth, in human form. She, Herself, said about Her exceptional and precious spiritual children: *"Immersed in meditation, the enlightened ones remain as they are, like wooden statues, for ages. When God needs them, He brings them down from their respective places. In this age of darkness, he brought Naren (Vivekananda) down from the realm of the Seven Rishis. His words are verily the words of the Vedas; they can never be untrue..."*

When God Asked, "Who Am I?"
The Day Satchitananda Wanted to Taste Its Own Sweetness

Once, Sri Ramakrishna heard a Brahmo Samaj preacher tell his congregation that "God was Dry." *"How can Brahman, who is the very essence of infinite sweetness, ever become dry?"* He exclaimed. At another time, the young Swami Vivekananda, Narendra, had begun to worship Radha as a knower of *Brahman*. People asked Sri Ramakrishna about this, and he stated: *"Once, Satchidananda wanted to taste divine bliss for Itself. So It created the wonderful Radhika. She was created from the divine person of Satchidananda Krishna. Satchidananda Krishna is the container, and He Himself, in the form of Radhika, is the contained. He manifested Himself in that way in order to taste His own Bliss, which is to say, in order to taste divine bliss by loving Satchidananda."*

Along with the Great Master's symbolic story about icebergs (God with form) dissolving into the ocean (of *Satchidananda*), this teaching about Sri Radha is especially effective in settling the unnecessary dispute between lovers of formlessness and those who prefer God with form (*Ishwara*). The human ego is obviously still in odious operation when arguments which covet personal perspectives are held, and narrow-minded stubbornness is adhered to.

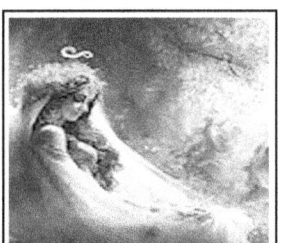

And perhaps this is why illumined souls hardly want to cast a glance upon most of humanity when they take embodiment. They will assist living beings who are open to being helped, to having their borders broadened, but do not want to involve themselves in the egoic games and foolish and futile contests they entertain. For, it is seen in this age that even followers of Christ have become one-sided and judgemental, and followers of Krishna have turned hypocritical and fundamentalist. Who can help such lost souls? The Great Master explained this phenomenon as well via a wonderful story from the tradition: *"Another story about Radha is that after her birth she would not open her eyes. She did not want to see any human being. But Yashoda came before her with baby Krishna in her arms. Then only would she open her eyes. In a playful mood, baby Krishna touched her eyes. Even today, young children in India touch each other's eyes with their fingers."* May all eyes be opened to the Truth by the Grace of the authentic Jesus and the original Govinda — who are Eternal Forms arising from the depths of the Ocean of *Satchidananda*.

Truth and the Moving Tirthas
One Yoga to See the Lord, Three to Help the World

When asked by the devotees about Yoga, Swami Vivekananda shed perfect light upon the subject. People would listen to him, then ask, "Sir, sometimes you extol the superiority of Bhakti, at other times Karma, and again, of Yoga (Raja)." He answered, *"The truth is this, that the knowledge of Brahman is the ultimate Goal, the highest destiny of man. But man cannot remain absorbed in Brahman all of the time. So he should perform selfless works to contribute to the real well-being of the people. But such are the intricacies of work that even great saints are caught in them and become attached. Good works, at the most, help purify the mind. About Bhakti, it is a slow process, but easy of practice. With Raja, if actual meditation (the seventh limb) is actually attained, progress can be made, but often the mind will be attracted to psychic powers and that will draw the practitioner away from attaining concentration upon one's true nature. Thus we see, that the path of Jnana is safest, of quick fruition, and the rationale of all other creeds, esteemed by all countries."*

Practice of the Four *Yogas*, though forgotten at times, is an ages-old tradition that helps living beings to remain in contact with God, especially if they be incarnating on earth over lifetimes. When devotion becomes sincere (*Bhakti*), and the mind has become stilled via meditation practices (*Raja*), then the aspirant can engage in service of God in mankind free of *karma*-causing errors, and thus make the best use of his time on earth. With *Jnanam*, however, it is said that, *"The knowers of Brahman become Brahman."* It is the only path that demands and utilizes sharp discrimination, and whose definitive end is the realization of Self as *Brahman*.

Thus, Vivekananda has stated, *"Only through Atmajnan is the world proven to be unreal, and when the world is finally seen to be unreal, then comes the key, freedom-delivering perception that, 'I am the only Reality.'"*

When living beings come to see the wonder of realized souls present right here on earth, they should know, in such rare cases, that *Brahmajnan* (Jnana Yoga) was already attained previously, before their birth. This is proven when it is seen that love for God (*Bhakti Yoga*) and deep meditation on God (*Raja Yoga*) is not a practice with them, but is being expressed naturally, throughout their lives. And if the question of the quickest way to realization came up in this context, and they would ask the swami, "Through what practice can I attain realization right away?" His response was, *"Gaining knowledge of the Self, the Atman, extolled so much in the scriptures, is gained in a thrice only by those who are moving Tirthas. They are seats of holiness from their very births."*

— *For more Godblogs go to community.srvwisdom.org*

◆ *Rabbi Rami Shapiro*

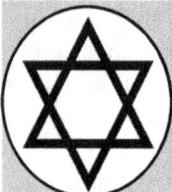

The Political Ideal in Judaism
The Brilliant Tactics of Both Holding & Restricting Power

Implicit in Judaism is a political ideal that, paradoxically, runs counter to the idea of politics. Politics is about power, specifically, the power of political elites to control other people's lives socially, economically, militarily, religiously, etc. The Jewish political ideal is anti-politics in that it is an effort to limit the power of elites, specifically the six elites dominant in ancient Israel: God, tribal chieftains, king, priesthood, Levites, and wealthy Israelites. What I will do in this essay is explore the ways Jews sought to limit the power of these elites, and in this way suggest an old/new politics for our own time.

The political ideal in Judaism can be gleaned from the two foundational texts of Judaism: TaNaKh, the 24 books of the Hebrew Bible written by hundreds of authors over a thousand years, and Talmud, the anthology of rabbinic ethics, law, customs, and Bible commentary compiled over 700 years from 200 BCE to 500 CE. Given the age of these texts we cannot expect to find within them a politics that reflects our modern liberal secular democratic sensibilities, but I believe we can find an ideal that can be reimagined for our own time.

Judaism is an ancient and on-going conversation with TaNaKH and Talmud. In defining Judaism this way, I am not ignoring *halacha* (Jewish law), *midrash* (Jewish lore), *mitzvot* (Jewish practice), or *minhaggim* (Jewish folkways). I'm only suggesting that all these claim authenticity by linking back to TaNaKH and Talmud. If we are going to uncover an authentic political ideal in Judaism it will have to be found in these two literary anthologies.

As I said, the Jewish political ideal is an effort to limit the power of the six elites dominant in ancient Israel: God, tribal chieftains, king, priesthood, Levites, and wealthy Israelites. Let me take up each one of these in turn.

Limiting the Power of God

In the Book of Genesis God establishes a covenant with all humankind through Noah:

"I establish my covenant with you with your descendants after you, and with every living creature that is with you — the birds, the livestock, and all the animals of the wild, all those that came out of the ark with you, every living being on earth." (Genesis 9: 9-10)

A covenant is an agreement between two parties, and the agreement God enters into is the promise never to destroy the world again. The interesting thing here is that there is no quid pro quo in Genesis 9. That is to say, while God agrees to limit God's power, Noah agrees to nothing. The author of Genesis 9 is setting limits on God's power, and God's power alone. This limitation of God's power is expanded in the story of Sodom.

In Genesis 18 God tells Abraham of the coming destruction of Sodom and all its inhabitants, the innocent along with the guilty. Rather than acquiesce to God's plan as Noah had done when informed of the impending flood and the untold deaths it would entail, Abraham challenges God saying, "How dare you kill the innocent along with the guilty! Should not the judge of all the earth deal justly?"

For God, might makes right, but for the author of Genesis 18 might must be placed in service to right, and right means not killing innocent people. Yes, God has the capacity to act unjustly and to slaughter the innocent along with the guilty, but Torah puts limits on that power; limits that are defined by humans — or at least one human, Abraham — rather than God.

Abraham teaches God what it means to be just: in this case not slaughtering the innocent along with the guilty. He then goes on to define justice by arguing with God over how many righteous

> "We have replaced the quest for justice with the quest for power. We have made a fetish of the state and allowed xenophobia to poison our policymaking. We have infected the idea of homeland with the wickedness of empire. We have replaced our skepticism of power with a lust for power, and our suspicion of government with a passion for influencing it. We have allowed the pain of the past to define who we are in the present and erase our hope of becoming something better in the future."

people living in a city are necessary for that city to be spared. Abraham starts with fifty and then bargains God into accepting only ten. If there are ten good people in a city the city must be spared. According to rabbinic commentary, Abraham stopped at ten assuming, incorrectly as it turned out, that Lot, his wife, his daughters, and his sons-in-law would be the saving ten — but our rabbis berate Abraham for not arguing for one: even the slaughter of a single innocent person is enough to make an act unjust. TaNaKh and Talmud are unabashed in curbing God's power, and placing it in service to justice as we humans define it.

Lo ba-Shamayim he

Perhaps the most striking limitation of God's power is set by Moses in the phrase *lo ba-shamayim* he, "It is not in heaven"; where the "it" is Torah herself. Moses is claiming that Torah and the human interpretation of Torah trump any revelation from God. In

> "Torah's teaching is that all people are created in the image of God (Genesis 1:26), and the idea that all Israel are the children of God. In the ancient Near East the king took the title Son of God for himself, but in Torah it is the people as a whole that are ranked as God's children: 'You are the children of YHVH your God;' (Deuteronomy 14:1) The king has no superior status and is not above the law, nor is his fate different from that of the common folk."

speaking to the Israelites about the godly path they are to follow, Moses says,

"For this teaching that I command you this day is not too difficult for you, nor is it far away from you. It is not in heaven that you shall excuse yourselves from doing it by saying, 'Who can ascend to the heavens and bring it to us, and explain it to us that we may act in accordance with it?' Nor is it on some distant shore that you excuse yourselves from doing it by saying, 'Who shall sail the oceans for us, and bring it to us, and explain it to us that we may act in accordance with it?' No! The teaching is very close to you: it is in your mouth; it is on your heart, that you may do it."

Moses is saying that the key to right living isn't outside you but inside you. And by extension he is instructing the people to heed their own capacity for reason even over divine revelation. The following teaching from the Talmud should erase any doubt that this is so.

Akhnai's Oven

There was a baker, a man named Akhnai, who sought a ruling as to the fitness of an oven he planned to use in his bakery. After examining the oven all but one of the rabbis voted against its use. Rabbi Eliezer, the lone dissenter, refused to give in saying, "If I am right, this carob-tree in our courtyard will prove it!" And in fact the tree jumped to the other end of the courtyard and replanted itself. The rabbis however were unimpressed, saying, "What does a carob-tree know about ovens?"

Rabbi Eliezer replied, "Then let the stream flowing in our courtyard prove I am right!" And at that the stream suddenly flowed backward. Again the rabbis were not persuaded, saying, "What does a stream know about ovens?"

Frustrated, Rabbi Eliezer said, "If I am right, let the walls of our study hall prove it." Immediately the walls began to collapse. Rabbi Joshua then leaped to his feet and spoke to the bricks, "What business is this of yours?" The bricks froze in place.

At his wits' end, Rabbi Eliezer shouted, "If I am right let God in Heaven proclaim it!" Whereupon God spoke to the rabbis saying, "Why do you argue with Eliezer? He is completely in the right!"

At that Rabbi Joshua again stood up, and lifting his face toward the heavens quoted the teaching of Moses saying, *"Lo bashamayim he!* It is not in heaven! You have given us Your Torah and taught us how to interpret it, and instructed us that we are to follow the will of the majority. That is what we have done. It is not for You to interfere!"

And what did God do in response to this rebuke? The Prophet Elijah who was with God at the time reports, God laughed with delight saying, "At last, at last, My children have defeated me! My children have defeated me!"

Not only does Judaism limit the power of God, Judaism imagines that God desires to have his power limited; in fact it is God's delight when we humans act godly without having to turn to God for guidance.

Limiting the Power of the Chieftains

In ancient times the tribal chieftains had the final word in matters of justice, and used their status to accrue power. But not in the Torah. While establishing justice as the focus of Judaism — *"Justice and only justice you will pursue!"* (Deuteronomy 16:20) — and after limiting God's power in this realm, Torah then strips the chieftains of judicial power by establishing a court system where the justices were chosen by the people themselves: *"Appoint judges and court officials throughout your tribes... and they shall render just decisions for the people."* (Deuteronomy 16:18)

Judges rather than tribal chieftains determine what is right and wrong, and they do so through an impartial court system run by officials of sterling character who cannot be bribed. (Deuteronomy 16:19) In cases where the judges are unclear as to just what is a righteous judgment they are to consult with the priests and the chief justice (Deuteronomy 17:9) but not with tribal chieftains.

Limiting the Power of Kings

When it comes to the power of the ruling class, Torah is explicit: *"Don't trust the princes,"* (Psalms 146:3), and the early rabbis even more so: *"Beware of the government, for rulers befriend you only for their own benefit. They pretend to be your friend when it suits them, but in your time of need they are nowhere to be found."* (Pirke Avot 2:3) Torah allows the people to establish a king for themselves, but the authors of Torah — having seen what happens when a king becomes God in other Near Eastern countries — restrict the power of the king to matters military and diplomatic, and then put limits on what the king can do in both those realms as well.

"One of your own community you may set over you as king... but he must not acquire many horses for himself, or return the people to Egypt in exchange for more horses... and he may not acquire many wives for himself... nor may he enrich himself with much silver and gold. When he has taken the throne of his kingdom, he shall have a copy of this law written for him in the presence of the priests. It shall remain with him and he shall read it every day of his life... diligently observing all the words of this law and these statutes, neither exalting himself above other members of the community nor turning aside from the commandment..." (Deuteronomy 17:14-20)

The limits placed on the king are not arbitrary. First, limiting the king's ability to amass large herds of horses, especially much-prized Egyptian horses, is Torah's way of limiting the king's ability to advance his military agenda since horses were used to pull chariots, supply wagons, and other military hardware.

Second, limiting the number of wives a king could have was Torah's way of limiting the diplomatic power of the king since marrying into the royalty of other nations was the way kings sealed treaties with those nations: the more wives a king had the larger his presence on the global stage, and the greater his influence and power. Limiting the number of wives a king may have limited the power he can wield.

Even with his military and diplomatic power curtailed, however, a king could still use his position to amass a personal fortune through political maneuvering, selling favors to wealthy patrons, and oppressive taxation of the people. Here too Torah steps in to limit the king's power by limiting the amount of wealth a king may accrue.

The reason why Torah can so dramatically limit the power of kings is due to Torah's teaching that all people are created in the image of God (Genesis 1:26), and the idea that all Israel are the children of God. In the ancient Near East the king took the title Son of God for himself, but in Torah it is the people as a whole that are ranked as God's children: *"You are the children of YHVH your God;"* (Deuteronomy 14:1) The king has no superior status and is not above the law, nor is his fate different from that of the common folk. (Deuteronomy 6:2; 10:12; 31:12) And because this is so, the king must function within the limits set by the people.

Limiting the Power of the Priesthood and Levites

Having curbed the power of God, chieftains, and kings, Torah turns her attention to the power of the priesthood and the tribe of Levi from which they come.

"The priests, the whole tribe of Levi, shall have no allotment or inheritance within Israel. They may eat the sacrifices that are the portion of YHVH, but they shall have no inheritance among the other members of the community; YHVH is their inheritance, as he promised them." (Deuteronomy 18:1-2)

Torah limits the power of the priests and Levites by making them landless in a civilization that is almost completely dependent on farming for its survival. They cannot grow their own food nor raise their own cattle. They are entirely dependent on the sacrifices the people bring to the Temple, meaning that the very survival of the priestly system, not to mention the priests and Levites themselves, is dependent upon the will of the people. If the priests and Levites cease to meet the needs of the people, and the people cease to bring their sacrifices to the Temple, the entire priestly edifice falls. Despite all the pomp and pageantry of priesthood, the power lies with the people.

Limiting the Power of the Financial Elites

The sixth elite Torah takes on is the wealthy Israelite, especially wealthy landlords who manage to take over lands once belonging to others. According to Joshua Berman in his book "Created Equal: How the Bible Broke with Ancient Political Thought in the ancient Near East":

"A peasant–a small landowner–resides on a small plot of privately owned lands, and engages in subsistence farming. As his margins of profit are slim, he can go into debt for any number of reasons: personal illness, crop failure, taxation, or the monopoly of resources by the state or private elite. His first line of recourse is to procure a loan, which he can only get at high interest. The high interest renders him insolvent, so he is forced to sell or deliver family members into debt-slavery, to pay off the debt. When this does not secure the means to pay off the debt, he has to resort to relinquishing or selling this own land–his means of production–and, finally to selling himself." (Berman, Joshua, Created Equal: How the Bible Broke with Ancient Political Thought. Oxford: Oxford University Press, 2008, p. 87)

What was true in general in the ancient Near East was true in ancient Israel as well. The primary economic engine of the time was the small family farm, and Torah sets forth a series of laws to protect it by limiting the power of wealthy landlords to gain permanent ownership of it.

First of all Torah takes on the usurpation of land and power by wealthy elites by denying land ownership to any human, and placing it in the hands of God alone:
- All the earth is Mine. (Exodus 19:5)
- The earth is YHVH's and everything in it. (Psalm 24:1)
- Behold the sky and the heavens beyond the sky belong to YHVH your God, as well as the earth and all that is found upon her. (Deuteronomy 10:14)

Second, a family farm cannot be sold in perpetuity, and must be returned to the family on the jubilee, (Leviticus 25:29-31) about which I will have more to say in a moment.

Third, clans are obligated to support members who have lost their land, their homes, and their livelihoods, and extended family members are prohibited from profiting off the suffering of the distressed family by loaning them money at interest or selling them food at a profit. (Leviticus 25:35-38)

And fourth, Even if things get so bad for a family that they have to sell themselves to other family members as slaves, they are not to be enslaved but are to be treated as hired servants and released from their servitude on the jubilee at which time *"they and their children shall be free from your authority; they shall return to their own family and to their ancestral property."* (Leviticus 25:39-41)

Limiting Power of Landlords

Of course not every family is going to fall into financial hardship, so Torah adds a series of laws limiting what successful farmers can do with their land. For example, the Book of Leviticus restricts the ability of farmers to lay claim to the entirety of their seasonal harvest.

"When you reap the harvest of your land, you may not reap to the very edge of your fields, nor may you reclaim any of the harvest dropped by your workers. These you must leave for the poor and the foreigners living among you." (Leviticus 23:22)

Chapter 25 of Leviticus introduces the injunction of the sabbatical year placing far more drastic limits on the farmer. Torah demands that once every seven years the earth is to lay fallow and no farming shall be done at all. During the sabbatical year the farmer is prohibited from sowing fields or pruning vineyards — *"the land is to have a year of rest."* (Leviticus 25:5)

"The farmer is further prohibited from harvesting for profit anything that grows of itself in the fields and vineyards, (Leviticus 25:5) and is obligated to use that produce to feed not only his family, but also male and female servants, and the hired worker and temporary resident who live among you, as well as your livestock and the wild animals in your land. Whatever the land produces may be eaten." (Leviticus 25:4-7)

No one is to go hungry during the sabbatical year, but no one is to make a profit either. So much for the ability of landowners to control their own land.

Immediately after this limitation of the power of the farmer over farmland, Torah speaks of a jubilee year that falls once every seven sabbatical years, or every 49 years.

"And you shall hallow the fiftieth year and you shall proclaim liberty throughout the land to all its inhabitants. It shall be a jubilee for you: you shall return every one of you to your property and every one of you to your clan." (Leviticus 25:10-11)

The year of jubilee is a time of resetting the economic balance scales. Given the contingencies of life as a subsistence farmer, artisan, or small business owner there is in no way to prevent economic inequality from emerging, but the jubilee year places a two-generation limit on its impact. If your grandparents were forced to sell the family farm, and if they were forced by necessity to sell themselves and your parents into debt-servitude, the jubilee means that this horror could not last more than 49 years, and that you would be freed from debt and your family farm would be returned to you.

Again, all of this harkens back to the principle that God rather than people owns the earth: *"The land shall not be sold in perpetuity, for the land is Mine; with Me you are all aliens and tenants."* (Leviticus 25:23)

Torah sought to establish a decentralized economic order that allowed for wealth accumulation without exploitation of the poor. By curbing the power of the economic elite, by insisting on the obligations of the extended family to care for everyone within it, and by insuring the return of ancestral properties every forty-nine years, Torah made sure that the society it established would be, at least by the standards of the time, fair and just, with poverty and extreme wealth being temporary states, and economic equality reestablished every two generations.

This system continues as the ideal through the prophetic and wisdom books of the Bible as well. Speaking to the elites of Israel, the prophet Ezekiel says, *"Thus says YHVH God: Enough, O Princes of Israel! Put a stop to your violence and oppression, and execute justice and righteousness instead. Cease to evict My people!"* (Ezekiel 45:9)

And the prophet Jeremiah says,

"Woe to you who builds your house by unrighteousness, and your upper rooms by injustice, who makes your neighbor serve you for nothing and does not pay wages due, who says, 'I will build myself a great house with spacious upper rooms,' who cuts out windows for it, paneling it with cedar and painting it with vermilion. Do you think you are a king because you compete in cedar? Did not your father eat and drink and do justice and righteousness? Then it was well with him. He saw to the welfare of the poor and needy; then it was well. Is not this to know Me? declares YHVH. But you have eyes and heart only for your dishonest gain, for shedding innocent blood, and for practicing oppression and violence." (Jeremiah 22:13-17)

The Jewish Political Ideal

Here then, is the Jewish political ideal:

By limiting the power of God Judaism ensures the survival of the planet and the rule of justice.

By limiting the power of the chieftains and placing courts in the hands of judges of sterling character, Judaism imagines a just society where justice rolls down like a mighty stream to sustain not only the powerful but the powerless (Amos 5:24) and where everyone acts justly and compassionately (Micah 6:8).

By limiting the power of kings Judaism envisions a world where weapons of war are repurposed as technologies for peace, and nations will neither go to war nor even study war (Micah 4:3).

By limiting the power of the priests and Levites, Judaism imagines a world without ecclesiastical tyranny where all peoples *"walk in the name of their gods"* (Micah 4:5). And:

By limiting the power of wealthy landlords, Judaism imagines a world where everyone sits unafraid on her own vineyard and farm (Micah 4:4); where everyone has sufficient food to eat and water to drink; where everyone has the opportunity to work at a job that brings them not only money but joy; and where friendship and love are honored as essential to the good life. (Ecclesiastes 2:24; 4:12)

Conclusion

When I look at the world today, I don't see this ideal in play anywhere, including the State of Israel. We have replaced the quest for justice with the quest for power. We have made a fetish of the state and allowed xenophobia to poison our policymaking. We have infected the idea of homeland with the wickedness of empire. We have replaced our skepticism of power with a lust for power, and our suspicion of government with a passion for influencing it. We have allowed the pain of the past to define who we are in the present and erase our hope of becoming something better in the future. This saddens me, but I am heartened by the ideal itself.

I believe in the power of ideals to remake society, and I believe that the political ideal in Judaism, especially when brought up to date with the liberal, secular, democratic, and egalitarian ideals of our age, is one that holds out promise for a just, kind, and peaceful world.

Rabbi Rami Shapiro is an award-winning author of over thirty-six books on religion and spirituality. He received rabbinical ordination from the Hebrew Union College-Jewish Institute of Religion and holds a PH.D. in religion from Union Graduate School. Rami co-directs the One River Foundation(www.oneriverfoundation.org), is a Contributing Editor at Spirituality and Health magazine where he writes the Roadside Assistance for the Spiritual Traveler column and hosts the magazine's podcast, Spirituality & Health with Rabbi Rami (www.spiritualityhealth.com).

◆ O.P. Sharma

THE MOTHERHOOD OF GOD
As Manifested In Sri Sarada Devi

*O Mother Supreme in human form
Granter of boons and bliss,
Distress of our souls removest Thou
And givest us contentment and bliss.
Thy children who offer all to Thee,
Do Thou makest them content and free.
O Great Mother of the Worlds,
be our salutations ever unto Thee.*

*O Sarada, Goddess propitious,
Killer of misery in souls resigned,
Savior of religion in every age,
By saints and sages worshipped,
O Mother kind.
Grant us love and wisdom, Thou,
O Grace Incarnate, to Thee we bow.*

Among the very few women who have been universally acknowledged as spiritual guides *par excellence* of all mankind, is, according to Wolfram H. Koch, Sri Ma Sarada Devi, the blessed divine consort of Sri Ramakrishna Paramahamsadeva. Observed the latter in regard to Her, "Had She not been so pure — without any trace of carnality in Her — it would not have been possible for me to successfully complete my sadhanas (which entailed complete and lifelong celibacy in thought, word and deed)."

Sri Ma Sarada Devi's following appears to be increasing day-by-day not only in India, but in many other parts of the world too. Recently, a Russian lady who visited Jaipur, informed us that Her life and teachings are being translated into the Russian language and are going to be published in Moscow. Also, many private Sri Ma Sarada Centres, devoted to Her ideas and ideals, have come into being in various countries. Actually, what draws people to Holy Mother is Her impressive mix of the divine and the human; of godliness and motherliness; of worldly, down-to-earth activities sublimated by lofty "practical" spirituality. There is no work, howsoever small or insignificant it may appear to be, She maintained, that cannot be elevated to the level of a spiritual exercise by the introduction of the "right approach and attitude." Even such a seemingly "petty" chore as sweeping the floor and after that putting away the broom, or the more "dignified" ones like cooking food in the kitchen and serving it, etc., can become "service of God" if they are seen and done in that light.

Sri Sarada Devi and Sister Nivedita

Also, viewing the human recipients of the service rendered not merely as friends, relatives, and so forth, but as "divinities incarnate," can become instrumental in one's own spiritual upliftment. As the Bhagavad Gita enjoins:

*Yatkarosi yaddashanasi yajjuhoshi dadati yat,
yattapasyashi Konteya tatkurushva madarpanam.*

In other words, all acts dedicated to God are so many forms of prayer and worship.

This lofty philosophy showed in every act of the Holy Mother. Her daily household chores, which mainly centered around serving the Master, Sri Ramakrishna Paramahamsadeva, and his disciples in various ways, evinced a constant feeling of the "presence of God," as Brother Lawrence would put it. Indeed, as all those who are acquainted with Her life and teachings will bear out, She was truth, purity, humility, holiness, compassion, and universality personified. Her whole life was an object lesson in spirituality.

In fact, as the Vedanta granthas rightly aver, it is only a person who *"dwells in Advaita"* (i.e., Oneness and its attendant universality) that can truly and on a lasting basis, be adorned with the aforementioned qualities and virtues as "natural ornaments." In other words, he/she does not have to make an effort to secure them; they, and many other virtues, come to the person concerned naturally. Such a person is "verily a living god (or, shall we say in this case, a living goddess?) on earth." To quote the views of Sister Nivedita (Margaret Noble, the famous

*"Holy Mother, Sri Ma Sarada Devi, was verily the Divine Mother of all;
She was a living testimony to the Motherhood of God."*

> "To me it has always appeared that She is Sri Ramakrishna's final word as to the ideal of Indian womanhood. But is She the last of an old order or the beginning of a new one?"

Western disciple of Swami Vivekananda), "Holy Mother, Sri Ma Sarada Devi, was verily the Divine Mother of all; she was a living testimony to the Motherhood of God."

Once somebody was ill-treating a cat in the presence of Sri Sri Ma, whereupon She restrained the individual from doing so, saying that by hurting the creature, he hurt Her too! At another time, some of her orthodox Brahmin relatives objected to Her treating a thief, named Amjad, so nicely. The latter, though a Muslim, reposed great faith in Her and used to occasionally visit the Ashrama to pay his respects to whom he called, "my Mother." True to Her nature, Sri Sri Ma brushed aside the objections of Her relatives, and said, "As Swami Saradananda (a disciple of Sri Ramakrishna) is my son (spiritually speaking), so is Amjad my son!"

No wonder Sister Nivedita, in her aforecited tribute, wrote about the living Goddess: *"To me it has always appeared that She is Sri Ramakrishna's final word as to the ideal of Indian womanhood. But is She the last of an old order or the beginning of a new one? In Her, one sees realised that wisdom and sweetness to which the simplest of women may attain. And yet, to myself, the stateliness of Her courtesy and Her great open mind are almost as wonderful as Her sainthood. I have never known Her to hesitate in giving utterance to a large and generous judgement, however new or complex might be the question put before Her. Her life is one long stillness of prayer."*

Sri Sarada Devi, the Holy Mother

Some years ago a swami of the Ramakrishna Order known to the present writer delivered a series of lectures in London on the "Motherhood of God" (to which concept now even the Pope at the Vatican has lent his seal of approval). At the end of the discourses, the speaker received a long-distance telephone call from an orthodox Christian gentleman who had heard about the subject of the lectures but could not reconcile himself to this novel idea. He incredulously asked the swami, "Does God have a gender? Can he be a woman?" To which the sannyasin retorted, "Why not! If God can be Father in heaven, why can't the same Almighty be Mother on earth, too? Why do you seek to put limits on what you call "Him?" Besides, the same Divine Personage can be totally impersonal — nameless, formless, genderless and attributeless. As Sri Ramakrishna points out in his Gospel, "God alone knows all that God is."

But the subject has deeper dimensions. Theological disputations apart, if you ask any child who does he prefer more, with whom does he feel more at home — father or mother — the answer, in most cases, is a foregone conclusion. The reason is, as the shastras say:

kuputro jayeta kwachidapi, kumata na bhavati.

In short, a child may become a delinquent, or *kaputa*, but a mother will always remain a mother — with her love, blessings, and forgiveness overflowing. That is why the tantras, in worshipping God as Mother, are hailed in the Hindu scriptures as *pancham Veda* — the fifth Veda.

We have seen above the example of how Holy Mother treated the errant thief, Amjad. On another occasion, when She showed great concern and solicitude for the welfare of a morally depraved woman, who nevertheless wanted to reform and had therefore approached Her for help and blessings, instead of turning this fallen woman away as many an orthodox Brahmin lady of those days would have done, Holy Mother took her by the hand and encouraged her to do everything she could to come back on the right path. To those who were somewhat taken aback by this concerned and compassionate behaviour of Hers towards the woman, Mother pointed out, *"If a child soils itself in dust and dirt, doesn't the mother pick it up and wash and clean it? Does she throw the child away?"*

In a sense, therefore, it may be said that Holy Mother's approach to the world at large, to all and sundry, is quite characteristic of Mother India who always extends a welcoming hand to all who wish to seek refuge in that ancient land. Mother India's salient philosophy down the ages has been to help others raise themselves spiritually and materially, subscribing as she does to the supremely enlightened notion of *atmavat sarvabhuteshu* — recognition of the one Self in all beings.

It is no wonder, then, that Swami Vivekananda observed with regards to Mother Sarada, *"To me, Mother's grace is a hundred thousand times more valuable than Father's. Mother's grace, Mother's blessings, are all paramount to me. Before proceeding to America I wrote to Mother to bless me. Her blessing came and at one bound I cleared the ocean."*

O.P. Sharma is a retired Lecturer in English from Govt. College, Ajmer (Raj.), India, at present actively engaged in the Ramakrishna-Vivekananda Movement in Rajasthan and is on the Managing Committee of Ramakrishna Mission, Jaipur. He has published a number of articles in Indian, British and American journals.

PRATITYASAMUTPADA
As Depicted Via The Twelve Nidanas in Buddhism

Pratityasamutpada is a title given by Lord Buddha to the spontaneous arising of mental phenomena in Samsara. Rendering the word into English brings up definitions such as "dependant origination," "conditioned genesis," "dependent co-arising," "interdependent arising, and others.

The Twelve Nidanas	Interdependent Arising
	(A Painful But Clarifying Example Of It In Daily Action)
1. Avidya, Ignorance	Go to the party, knock on the door, do not know anyone there, no reference point, freeze, go numb, experience self-consciousness
When ignorance is the condition, mental formations arise	
2. Samskara, Impressions	Cannot just hang out at the door, must do something, look for safe reference point, head for the bar
When samskaras are the condition, consciousness arises	
3. Vijnana, (external) Consciousness	Now oriented to the party, need nourishment, become aware of an oral fixation, pour yourself a drink
When consciousness is the condition, name and form arise	
4. Namarupa, Name and Form	Feel warmth in the body, feel fortified, empowered, and more expansive
When name and form are the condition, the 5 senses arise	
5. Sadayatana, the Five Senses	Survey the situation, look for someone to talk to
When the five senses are the condition, contact occurs	
6. Sparsha, Contact	See someone interesting who catches your eye
When contact is the condition, feeling arises	
7. Vedana, Feeling/Emotion	Person looks good, attractive, worthy of our attention, we feel good
When feeling is the condition, craving arises	
8. Trsna, Craving	Desire to talk to them, engage them, irresistible impulse, so lonely
When craving is the condition, clinging arises	
9. Upadana, Clinging	Mind is fixated on how to approach them, can't ignore them, already caught
When clinging is the condition, being arises	
10. Bhava, Being	Go over to talk to the person, yak, yak, yak
When being is the condition, birth arises	
11. Jati, Birth	Get to know the person, give birth to a relationship
When birth is the condition, aging and dying arise	
12. Jaramarana, aging and death	Endless conversation, focus starts to flag, diffuse, interrupted, reference point dies, gap, no one to talk to
When aging and dying in ignorance is the condition, rebirth in ignorance occurs.	
1. Ignorance	Panic, go numb again, aloneness sets in
2. Impressions	Head back for the bar for another drink…etc…

(Humorous Description Courtesy of Douglas Penick)

The Chain of Rebirth With Its 12 Links (Nidanas) In Buddhism

(Three Lifetimes)

Nidanas 1 & 2 — The Previous Existence

Avidya — Ignorance
Failure to affirm the suffering-ridden nature of existence and renounce it

Samskaras — Mental Impressions
Subtle deposits from physical, verbal, and psychological actions form in the mind

Nidanas 3 — 8 — Conditioning of the The Present Existence

Vijnana — Relative consciousness
Awareness gets crystallized by previous life-experiences and enters wombs

Namarupa — Name & Form
A fresh body is formulated based upon past impulses and impressions

Shadayatana — The Six Bases
Experiences springing from exposure to the realms of the senses develop more karma

Sparsha — Contact/Relations
Interminging with the world, its peoples, and its objects contributes to karmic conditioning

Vedana — Sensation
Continual and repeated stimulation of body and senses adds further conditioning

Nidanas 8 — 10 — Fruits/Effects of the The Present Existence

Trishna — Craving/Desire
Desire for futher contact of senses with objects arises in order to gain satisfaction

Upadana — Attachment
Selfish clinging to sense-life enmeshes the mind deeper in embodied existence

Bhava — A New Birth
Due to decay of the old body, the desire for a new body arises

Nidanas 11 & 12 — The Future Existence

Jati — Rebirth
Passage from birth to death occurs under karmic circumstances, resulting in another body

Jara-maranam — Old Age & Death
After life and passage from the new body, life gets perpetuated in another body

Copyright 2017, Babaji Bob Kindler

ADVAITA-SATYAM-AMRITAM

Fifty-Eight Verses of Encomium to the Excellence of Self-Effort

Before entering into the play of relativity and multiplicity
via the Four States of Consciousness,
the Mother of Wisdom reminded me of
the Two Who are One, and I meditated on Them devoutly.

Then, while associating with the body, the Two Limiting
Powers of Maya beset my mind and senses
but I remembered the Divine Mother of the Universe
and rested in Her Two Priceless Jewels.

Upon opening my eyes on the universe, the Three Worlds
appeared magically, enticing me with promise.
I took refuge in the Two Highest Supreme Blessings
and was still and content.

Wondering at the nature of these worlds and their offshoots,
I came to know of the Three Eternal Gateways.
Abandoning unrighteousness, I resorted to the
Two Kinds of Knowledge and attained the Four Fruits of Life.

Coming to know of people's attachment to lower knowledge,
I perceived Two Types of Ego. Seeking maturity,
I plunged into the Two Great Philosophical Streams
to be free of ownership and agency.

Moving about in wonder, the Threefold Miseries
next revealed their various pitfalls to me,
but the Ultracosmic Trinity came forth and saved me
as I performed the Three Alluring Offerings.

This vision opened new eyes and I looked at humanity
and saw the Four Conditions of Embodied Beings.
Compassionately noting all who suffer, I gratefully perceived
the Four Kinds of Virtuous Aspirants, and joined them.

Shortly thereafter, I met my incomparable Guru
who described to me the Three Designations of Aspirants.
Conferring upon me the Three Necessary Prerequisites
to Spiritual Life, he established me formally in the sacred path.

Almost immediately, the Three Obstacles to Self-Realization
loomed before me in intimidating fashion,
but so did the Three Transformations of Consciousness in Yoga,
which I swiftly took refuge in.

Next, I noticed the Nine Complacencies
that persist in the minds of worldly beings and novitiates,
and uncovered a profound solution
by following the Nine Levels of Awareness in Aspirants.

Early along the superlative way, my gracious Guru came forward
again to warn me about the Sixteen Evolutes of Maya.
I perceived them prevalent throughout relativity and got free
by studying the Ten Fundamental Tenets of Samkhya.

Thereafter, the Eleven Main Characteristics of Maya
were rendered clear to my intelligence.
This knowledge inspired me to recite
the Twenty Truths of Truth daily with heartfelt devotion.

Due to barriers like the Nine Distractions in Spiritual Life,
doubt about my Guru arose in my mind,
but this was swiftly put to death when I heard
of the Four Qualities of an Authentic Spiritual Teacher.

Shame at my lack of faith in the Guru made me aware
of the presence of the Eight Fetters in human nature,
so I quelled them methodically by engaging in
the Triple Tenet of Kriyayoga and other salient practices.

As I began to sport in the various lokas, the Three Chains of
Transmigration cast their shackles towards me.
so my illumined Preceptor transmitted to me the teaching
of the Three Kinds of Purity, to ensure my freedom.

At the lowest of the Three Stages of Mental Evolution
my mind experienced doubt and foreboding.
But the Four Kinds of Worship and the Four Ways
of Perceiving God prevailed and transported me higher.

Sedulously, I engaged the power of analysis
and reasoned well in my mind about the Five Sheaths,
and then happily detached from them using the
Two Methods of Discrimination indicated by my teacher.

Intensifying my analysis of mind and matter,
I came upon the teaching of the Four Illusory Bodies.
Perceiving its stultifying nature, I mentally dissolved all four
utilizing the Four Sentinels of Spiritual Life.

Then, the pernicious Three Enemies of Reason
sprung up to challenge me, seemingly out of nowhere.
I studied the Three Proofs of Truth and the
Three Stages of Philosophy and these enemies fled in terror.

Attempting to fathom the depths of the Six Darshanas,
my mind balked, and my Guru came to my rescue again.
The Three Qualities of the Scriptures and Three Techniques
for Interpreting the Scriptures brought me clarity.

Studying scripture, I was fascinated by the
Twenty-four Cosmic Principles and the Twelve Higher Tattvas,
and became awed to find them all expressed
through The Four Manifestations of the Word.

While attempting to master the Seven Levels
of Advanced Knowledge, I fell short and balked.
My Guru reminded me of the Ten Conditions of the
Guru/Disciple Relationship and inspired me on to the goal.

As love and gratitude bubbled up blissfully within me,
I was made aware of the Nine Limbs of Bhakti,
and thereafter was vouchsafed the practice
of the Eight Devotional Aids to realize them.

While contemplating the Six Transformations of Relative
Existence, my mind became temporarily irresolute,
so I swiftly recalled the Seven Steps to the Attainment
of Kaivalya and reached blessed transcendence.

Next, the disconcerting appearance of the Triple Illusion
duly challenged my mind's perception,
but I pierced and shattered it coursing blissfully along
the Three Plateaus of Spiritual Evolution.

The appearance in the mind of the Fourteen Worlds, seven
higher and seven lower, once caused me incertitude.
By comprehending the Four Clarities and the Five
Atmospheres of Existence, I dissolved them into their Source.

Seeking freedom from all illusions, I entered into the practice
of the Four Steps to Fundamental Detachment,
only to find to my amazement that there were
Twelve Levels of Dispassion listed in the scriptures.

Looking back, I remember well when I became acutely aware
of the Two Directions Of The Mind-Stream.
And I recall as well the precious Guru affirming the true way
with the Three Powerful Practices of Vedanta.

On one occasion, the Four Veiled Pathways
dubiously presented themselves before my tentative mind,
I swiftly initiated the Fourfold Formula for
Success in Spiritual Life and easily transcended them forever.

Then, observing the worldly, the Four Fundamental Paths of
Life revealed the potential choices for all living beings.
I refused the first, transcended the second, practiced
the Four Yogas and reached nondualism straightaway.

The practice of Yoga made me aware of Five Types of Yogis,
and I noticed how the first three fail the goal.
Resolving not to end up in this predicament, I applied myself
to achieve the Four Levels of Yogic Attainment.

When the Three Stupifactions threatened to influence
my contented life and peaceful mind,
the Four Sensitivities came to my rescue
and I thankfully tread the way of the Wise.

And no sooner did the Three Types of Karma, the Three
Gunas, and the Five Cosmic Bondages approach,
then I quickened the pace of my inner journey
by way of the Seven Victories of Involution.

Searching within to gain more strength
in order to succeed in the Nine Steps to Perfection,
I came auspiciously upon the Four Perfections of the Heart
which benefitted me immensely.

Predictably, both the Six Passions and
the Four Deadly Traps came looking for me as well,
but my Guru had earlier blessed me with the
Four Treasures and Six Jewels, so what harm could befall me?

The Five Pranas became restless and unruly
at one point in my concentrated sadhana,
but those and other problems were alleviated
via the Seven Methods For Attaining Mastery of Awareness.

The Four Causes of Distraction then tried to enter
and occupy my body, mind and life-force,
but the Ten Prerequisites to the Practice of Yoga I wielded
were too much for them, and they died away.

Fortunately, the Five States of the Mind-field
were shown to me in a vast firmament of precious teachings.
I transcended the first three, attained quiescence of mind,
and rested resolutely in the Fifth.

The Four Erroneous Views once infringed
upon my deep and lucid thinking process,
A solution quickly presented itself
through practice of the Four Beneficial Attitudes.

The well-known Four Obstacles to Meditation
also rose up early in my contemplative practice,
and fell down immediately due to practice of the Five Aids
to Steadiness of Mind taught to me by my spiritual teacher.

Awareness of the Six Billows and Six Transformations
once gave me considerable cause for trepidation,
but they were no match for the wondrous
Thirteen Inherent Characteristics of the Atman I discovered.

The Four Paths of Transmigration After Death
seemed to hold no allowable place for me.
This was confirmed as I practiced the Nine Step Process
of Meditation on AUM as given by the beloved Guru.

In the illimitable realm of the Divine Word,
I wisely initiated the Three Elements of Mantra Practice,
and succeeded wonderfully thereby
while duly exercising the Four Types of Japa Practice.

Later, the Seven Malas of Maya tried to insinuate themselves
on my precious sempiternal existence.
Then, the Three Conditions of Mature Detachment
graced my mind, and I pierced Maya immediately.

*Along the pathway of my life, the Three Types of Bondage
came forth as if to capture my mind and spirit,
but that was short-lived, for I discovered and implemented
the Three Kinds of Liberation thereafter.*

*While practicing the Five Types of Sacrifice,
I blenched at the many inferior births possible in this life,
but gained relief with gratitude and celerity
upon remembering the Four Auspicious Boons.*

*In the course of my mind-revivifying spiritual practice,
the Five Obstacles to Yoga posed me difficulties.
I merely intensified my practice of
the Three Treasures of Patanjala and
the Eight Limbs of Yoga.*

*At an advanced level of practice, the Three Obstacles to
Attaining Mature Detachment impeded my progress.
I resorted to pursuing the Eight Great Accomplishments
and broke this triple barrier down completely.*

*The Seven Stages of Higher Wisdom
dawned on my awareness at a deeper level of sadhana,
and I found they led me to an ebullient confirmation
of the Four Divine Affirmations, called Mahavakyas*

*I heard with awe about the recondite system
of the Seven Chakras from my spiritual teacher.
He transmitted esoteric information on the Four Yogas
of Kundalini Yoga and I devoutly embraced the Tantra.*

*In this esoteric path, the Twenty Yamas and Niyamas
According to Tantra became known to me,
and having practiced them all, the Twenty-four Symbologies
of Goddess Kali dawned on my mind.*

*Inspired by the path, I exerted profusely in order to master
the Seven Qualifications of a Tantric Aspirant,
and gradually the Six Signs of Awakening Kundalini
appeared in me and I tasted samadhi.*

*Due to this, my perception was heightened,
and I yearned to hear of the Five Divine Seats of the Devi.
My illumined preceptor informed me of
the Four Aspects of Shakti and I experienced Her darshan.*

*As bliss turned into realization, the Five Main Aspects
of the Divine Mother manifested before me.
Thus, Mother taught me pure devotion and also revealed
the Five Divine Moods for Worshipping God.*

*Eschewing the mind's tendency towards limitation,
I acknowledged all the Five Main Religious Paths of India.
No sooner did I attain this universal view than
the Nine Durgas danced ecstatically before my inner vision.*

*Meditating on the Ten Divine Articles of Sri Durga
which She holds in Her beautiful hands,
I became aware of the Six Treasures of the Godhead
which transmuted my mind's dross to pure gold.*

*I contemplated with wonder the Ten Meditations
on the Nature of Brahman in the scriptures.
My Guru noticed my devotion and instructed me
in the Seven Types of Meditation, conferring liberation.*

*Meditating on my immutable Self, called Atman,
the Six Proofs of Purusha were revealed to me.
I realized then what the ancient rishis knew —
the Ten Immutables of Paramatman —
and entered ecstatic absorption.*

Om Shanti, Shanti, Shantih — Om Peace, Peace, Peace.

This Encomium, excerpted from "The Sword of the Goddess" manuscript by Babaji Bob Kindler, forms a list of some of the many beneficial spiritual disciplines presented and explained in that book that have emerged throughout the history of Eastern religious tradition. In this expansive terrain of teachings are found the keys to all doorways leading to the numerous chambers of Insight and Self-realization. For the sufferer, the seeker, the aspirant, the attained, and the adept alike, this anthology of Divine Mother's Wisdom methods will provide all that is tangible, practical, instructive and inspiring, thus removing the impositions of ignorance and suffering.

Study the Encomium directly via email with Babaji Bob Kindler through SRV's *Ashram of the Subtle Realms,* a membership community of serious spiritual aspirants.
Visit **community.srvwisdom.org**
Be our guest for a month.

Additionally,
SRV's Assistant Dharma teachers conduct an ongoing study of the Encomium every other Wednesday.
Learn more at **srvinfo@srv.org**

Wisdom Facets From The Garland of Universality

"Mankind ought to be taught that religions are but the varied expressions of The Religion which is Oneness, so that each may choose the path that suits him best."

Swami Vivekananda

"I have fashioned a garland of the different religious traditions of the world, and have offered them all at the sacred Feet of the Mother of the Universe."

Sri Ramakrishna Paramahamsa

"When ahimsa, the incapacity to harm others, and dharma, the inherent goodness dwelling in the heart, are fully developed in man, then he is said to have attained Enlightenment."

"Meditate deeply and reach the Great Source. Branching streams cannot compare to It. Then, sitting in utter silence, as the heavens turn and the earth is upset, you will not even wink."

"The two primal spirits, who reveal themselves in vision as twins, are the better and the bad, in thought, word, and action. Between these two the wise ones choose aright; the foolish, not so."

"A tall tree is at first a slender shoot. A tall tower is raised by placing a few stones atop one another. Journeys of many leagues begin with a single step. Be careful of your thoughts; they are the beginning of your deeds."

"Of old, heaven and earth were one, like an egg containing seeds. The pure part was drawn out to form heaven; the gross part became earth. Heaven formed first, earth thereafter. Divine beings were produced between them."

"Who is the wise man? Whosoever is constantly learning from others. Who is the rich man? Whosoever is contented with his lot. Who is the strong man? Whosoever is capable of self-mastery."

"Thou shalt hear what no ear has heard, thou shalt see what no eye has seen, and at last thou shalt come into that sacred Presence and thou shalt find only one sole Being in place of the world and its mortal creatures."

"And I turned within to behold wisdom, as well as madness and folly. Then I saw that wisdom excelled folly, as far as light excels darkness, and I invested myself with Her as a raiment of glory and put Her on my head as a crown of joy."

SRV Associations 2024 Dharma Visits to
NE Portland, OR | Camas & Stevenson, WA

SRV Associations 2024 Three In-Person Retreats

For details: srvinfo@srv.org | www.srv.org

May 2024
May 22	Wed	7:00pm	**Topics in Vedanta**, NE Portland, OR
May 24	Fri	4:00pm	**Arrive at Windwood Waters for Retreat**
May 28	Tue	12noon	**Retreat ends** (Stevenson, WA)
May 29	Wed	6:00pm	**Arati & Satsang**, Camas, WA Shrine

RSVP at srvinfo@srv.org to receive directions

Memorial Weekend Retreat at Windwood Waters
NonDuality In Vedanta & Buddhism:
Gaudapada's Karika & Tilopa's Mahamudra
Friday, May 24th - Tuesday, May 28th, 2024

September 2024
Sep 4	Wed	7:00pm	**Topics in Vedanta**, NE Portland, OR
Sep 6	Fri	4:00pm	**Arrive at Windwood Waters for Retreat**
Sep 10	Tue	12noon	**Retreat ends**
Sep 11	Wed	6:00pm	**Arati & Satsang**, Camas, WA Shrine

RSVP at srvinfo@srv.org to receive directions

September Retreat At Windwood Waters
The World's Great Mother Scripture
Friday, September 6 - Tuesday, Sep 10, 2024

December 2024
Dec 11	Wed	7:00pm	**Topics in Vedanta**, NE Portland, OR
Dec 13	Fri	4:00pm	**Arrive at Windwood Waters for Retreat**
Dec 17	Tue	12noon	**Retreat ends**
Dec 18	Wed	6:00pm	**Arati & Satsang**, Camas, WA Shrine

RSVP at srvinfo@srv.org to receive directions

Winter Retreat at Windwood Waters
Sankhya's Tattva Samasa Sutras:
Sankhya's Crucial Place Among the Six Darshanas
Friday, Dec 13 - Tuesday, Dec 17, 2024

Suggested Donation for public events: $20. No one turned away.

Stay Informed about SRV Classes, Retreats, & Online Seminars.
Sign our email list & Explore SRV Offerings

Become a Member of SRV Wisdom
SRV's online "Ashram of the Subtle Realms"
and be our guest for a month.
Community.srvwisdom.org

In-Person Retreats with Babaji Bob Kindler

Join us for the Peace-conferring atmosphere of Divine Wisdom & Devotion: classes on Divine Wisdom, its application, engaging formal and informal satsangs, & devotional music with Babaji and students.

Memorial Weekend Retreat at Windwood Waters — **May 24 - 28**
Nonduality in Vedanta & Buddhism
Gaudapada's Karika & Tilopa's Mahamudra
Near Stevenson, WA

The precious teaching of Nonduality is known to a rare, few souls. Throughout time it has remained incomprehensible to parents and ancestors, even dharmic ones. Religion in this world, being either fundamentalistic or dualistic, overlooks it entirely. Educational systems, even at the collegiate level, rarely hear of it or offer it for study. Finally, the world's philosophies, fail to perceive its import. At this retreat, be among those who will hear of it in two of its most mature forms available today, via direct instructions on how to work it into life and mind.

September Retreat at Windwood Waters — **Sept 6 - 10**
The World's Great Mother Scripture

The wisdom of Sri Durga and Her various Goddess forms will be transmitted by consulting and studying the world's greatest Divine Mother scripture, The "Srimad Devi Bhagavatam." The guru's long-standing study and communion with this powerful scripture will afford students the opportunity to imbibe rare expressions of Indian Dharma and Nonduality – straight from the Source, Herself.

December Retreat at Windwood Waters — **Dec. 13 - 17**
Sankhya's Tattva Samasa Sutras:
Sankhya's Crucial Place Among the Six Darshanas

Within the 25 slokas of this ancient scripture, not only are the timeless principles of Purusha and Prakriti described comprehensively, but teachings concerning the nature of suffering and its origin (taught by Lord Buddha thousands of years later) are taken up. Nature's unmanifested side, followed by the appearance and influence of the subtle drivers of evolution, and other familiar but usually unsourced teachings are present there, and thus rise fortuitously for deep contemplation. Here is an opportunity to hear and study India's foundational philosophy, which gave breadth and depth to systems as mature and powerful as Vedanta and Buddhism, and which broadened the darshana of Yoga and all systems of Shaivism as well.

SRV Associations 2024
Online Weekend Seminars with Babaji Bob Kindler

Two full days of classes on the Wisdom of Mother India & engaging satsangs with Babaji and students.

Seminar 1 — **March 16 & 17**
Establishing a Spiritual Life in Materialistic Times
Connecting Prana, Psychic Prana, & Intelligence to Shakti

Beings on earth, for the most part, have a work life, a social life, and a family life. Some even have a religious life. Possessing a spiritual life, however, is extremely rare, and that is because most all of humanity's connections flow outwards into matter. One might aver that human thought is inward, but the brains of most beings harbor thoughts about matter only. Their plans, their dreams, their imaginings, their aspirations, even their prayers, all involve material objects. Then, nothing purely spiritual in nature can take root in them, except, as the seers tell them, their own True Nature.

One's True Nature is desireless; It has no wants. It is actionless; It is free of the sense of agency. It is beyond the realm of thought; It does not project or create. This is why the ancient seers of many religions separated Spirit from Matter, God from Mammon. But those inner avenues walked by them into the realm of Divine Reality are blocked today. We do not breathe in higher Awareness, nor think in terms of higher visions. The Mother of our thoughts and intelligence is not loved, cherished, or ardently sought after. Humanity's precious Life-force has come to a standstill and gelled in the dark valley of material objects, far short of the opening to the blessed Citadel of the Heart. It must flow again, and reach Her.....

Seminar 2 — **June 29 & 30**
The Names of The Lord & The Wisdom of the Mother
Mantra Yoga's Intimate Relationship with Jnana Yoga's Wisdom Transmission

Among spiritual ideals, the best is an exemplar. Amidst practices, the best is that of mantra. When the mantra is received from an exemplary guru, both karmas and future lifetimes swiftly become a thing of the past. Further, as mantra practice matures over time, it inevitably befriends that best of destroyers of ignorance called Jnanam. Thus, the secret of an exemplary guru is that he/she delivers the mantra to the ready aspirant in a timely fashion, and it is loaded with wisdom that is set to infuse the human mind like a slow release medicine in the bloodstream.

Similar to Vedanta and the classic 8-Limbed Yoga in philosophical systems, then, Mantra Yoga and Jnana Yoga are one of the best of spiritual hybrids in the realm of spiritual practice. The unique way in which they both grow and work together will be inspected and explored in this seminar.

Seminar 3 — **August 3 & 4**
From Dreams Awake, From Bonds Be Free
What Happens to Consciousness in Deep Sleep

Often presented to spiritual aspirants either in the form of a guru's instructive interpretation of dreams, or as an illusion of the mind which the soul is attempting to awaken from, the dream state, called *svapna* in Sanskrit and Vedanta, both supplies the waking state with its objects, and facilitates the individual's (ego's) smooth passage into *Sushupti*, or deep sleep. Deep Sleep, in turn, is both a potential precursor to nondual Samadhi, and a storehouse of subtle seeds for all the "dream-stuff" of the mind, or its *chitta*. These unwatered seeds later become thoughts which produce solid objects in the waking state (*jagrat*).

This fascinating way of inner perception given to us by illumined Indian seers such as Gaudapada, termed the "Three States of Consciousness," reveal the mind's unique ability to produce all things out of its internal fabric of awareness, and also fill in philosophical gaps in today's spotty understanding of the truth of Nonduality. Along with *Turiya* — That what lies beyond the "Three States" (Formless Reality) — we can behold the human mind's role in God's magnificent Divine Sport, availing our understanding of what is called "The Four Feet of *Brahman*," or how God gets from place to place in the worlds of name and form in time and space.

Seminar 4 — **October 5 & 6**
A Revealing Look at Birth, Life, Death, and Rebirth
Fulfilling the Soul's Transmigration, and Ending It

As the blessed poet/saints of India often sing, to incarnate across the boundless expanse of Nature's five elements is a difficult task for the transmigrating soul. One's formless Essence, *Atman*, or *Prajnaparam*, does not transmigrate, but as long as the individual's mind holds karmic residue from past lifetimes, so long will it need to take births in relativity to dissolve it. Then only is it free from rebirth.

Becoming aware of the relative truth of rebirth launches one on the path to liberation from taking on forms, particularly with regard to assuming them in ignorance. Then, tracing the soul's travels through a host of worlds and forms, followed by applying effective disciplines in order to disintegrate the tendencies and conditionings inherited there, will avail the soul of the subtle techniques that will introduce it to the salient truth of liberation (*jivanmukta*), and the final realization of its eternal oneness with Formless Reality (*Brahman*). As the Father of *Yoga* states: *"She, the primordial Shakti, strips away the overlays of name and form from the aspiring being, and returns it to its final emancipation."*

Learn More at srvinfo@srv.org | www.srv.org>retreats

A Ground-Breaking Interfaith Program

In the Spirit Interviews with Lex Hixon

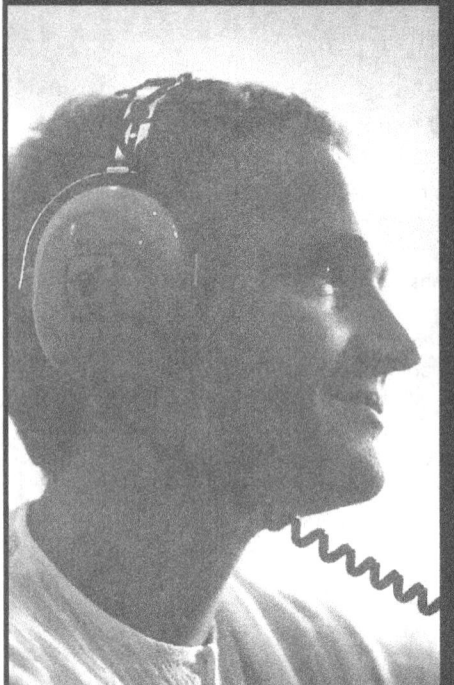

From the early 1970's through the late 1980's, Lex Hixon hosted **In the Spirit** from WBAI, in NYC. As a list, the fruit of this selfless work reads like a comprehensive Who's Who of the spiritual, artistic and intellectual heart and mind of both Eastern and Western cultures. Over 300 programs can be downloaded at www.srv.org

- Kalu Rinpoche
- Sakya Trizin
- Dudjom Rinpoche
- Tartan Tulku
- Trungpa Rinpoche
- Bernie Glassman
- Master Shen Yen
- Rebbi Gedalia
- Rabbi Zalman Schachter
- Rabbi Dovid Din
- Sheikh Muzafer
- Guru Bawa
- Pir Vilayet Khan
- Swami Muktananda
- Meher Baba
- Sri Chinmoy
- Ram Das
- Swami Rama
- Mother Teresa
- Father Daniel Barrigan
- Programs on Meister Eckhart, Padre Pio, Mother Mary, Jesus Christ
- Programs on Sri Ramakrishna, Divine Mother, Ramana Maharishi, Sri Aurobindo

Hearing
about Brahman is good.

Taking teachings
on Brahman is better.

Meditating directly
on Brahman is better still.

But best of all
is that meditation in which all doubt about the nature of Reality dies away forever.

—Shankaracharya's
Crest Jewel of Discrimination

Dharma Weekends at SRV Associations

Online & in-person with
Babaji Bob Kindler, Spiritual Director

Satsang
Join us for Q & A
Bring your questions
from classes and studies

Saturdays
at 8:00am HST
Online

Brahman Bytes
Group Philosophical
Discussion

Saturdays
at 10:00am HST on
community.srvwisdom.org

Sunday Class
Vedanta, Yoga, Tantra

Sundays
at 2:30pm HST
Online & in person

Schedule Subject to Change | Sign up for schedule emails: srv.org

Dharma Art Wisdom Charts
www.dharmaartwisdomcharts.com

SRV Websites:
www.srv.org
community.SRVWisdom.org
www.nectarofnondualtruth.org

Order Dharma Charts for your:
Meditation Room • Yoga Studio
Temple • Classroom • Home • Office

Bring the Light of Wisdom into Conversations.

Discuss Dharma with your Children, Friends, Co-Workers, Relatives, & Students

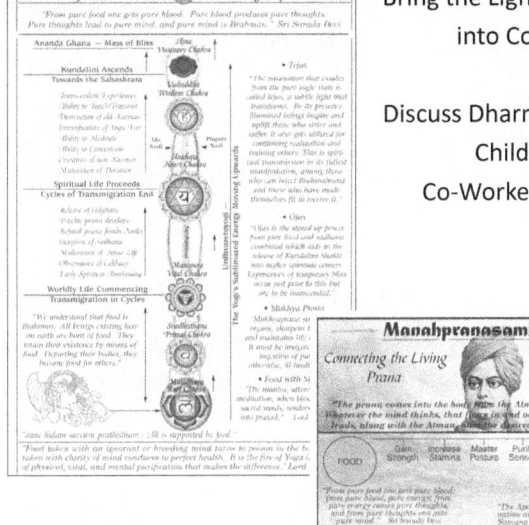

Archival Ink
Full Size: 2' x 3'
Ready to frame

Explore Mother India's Timeless Wisdom

www.srv.org
- Sanskrit Chants to Learn & Practice
- "In the Spirit" Audio Interviews
- Teachings for Youth/Children
- Articles on SRV Ideals, Teachers, & Wisdom
- Sacred Books & Music online store
- This website is the hub for everything SRV....

Join the Ashram of the Subtle Realms:
community.SRVWisdom.org
- Spiritual Community
- Easy access to: live classes, archived video and audio classes
- Nectar of Non-Dual Truth back issues
- Special discounts for books, charts, and a retreat of your choice.

Nectar of Non-Dual Truth—A Journal of Universal Religious & Philosophical Teachings
www.nectarofnondualtruth.org
- Learn about Nectar's mission
- Preview upcoming articles and writers
- Order back issues

Dharma Art Wisdom Charts—For the Study of Wisdom
Dharmaartwisdomcharts.com
- Beautiful, essential Wisdom charts for Home, School, Spiritual Center, and Yoga Studios.
- Archival inks, ready to frame

YouTube Channel Class Series with Babaji Bob Kindler
Youtube.com/user/SRVAssociations
- Mother's Path of Nonduality
- God/Brahman Reflected in the Universe
- Non-Touch Yoga of Gaudapada
- The Third Eye & Kundalini's 7 Chakras
- Spiritual Interviews
- Satsangs, Sacred Music Videos, & more

ADVAITA-SATYAM-AMRITAM

Comments about Nectar from our Readers

"I have searched for some time and finally found Nectar. Where in all the world, especially in the wake of all the health and hatha-oriented magazines springing up, can one find a journal like it? Nectar heals by revealing our eternal inner Wellness. It is a testament to truth in a world addicted to half-truths. Its voice is desperately needed."

"This magazine is the only magazine my mind can truly connect to on a deep and meaningful level. I could really go on and on about how refreshing it is to have the truth and profound wisdom this Magazine shares. So much dilution out there and NO other magazine compares (I have "tried" them all I think)" Sandy Hicks, Grounded by Yoga

"I very much appreciate your detailed presentation of Advaita Vedanta, Sri Ramakrishna, and Mother Kali. I hope it will reach a large number of American Citizens."

President Maharaj, Ramakrishna Order Swami Ranganathananda

"I'm dazzled by a tradition that truly acknowledges the deepest held truths held by different religions and I know that this is a rare thing. I am delighted to find the pearls of wisdom shared in this journal from other traditions such as Judaism, Sufism, Buddhism, Hinduism, Vedanta, Islam, etc., acknowledged and held high along with the truths of SRV's Tradition."

Sacred Music from Hawaii

Jai Ma Music
The Music of Babaji Bob Kindler

Chanting • Instrumental • Devotional • Poetry

Kali Bol Ramakrishna
Gita Govinda Mala
Hari Om Ramanam
Guru Bhajans
Jai Ho Vivekananda!
Siva! Siva!
Hymns to the Goddess
Shakti Bhajans
Deva Devi Svarupaya
Kali Bol
Sarada Ramakrishna Name
Hymns to the Master & Mother
108 Names of Sarada
Universal Aspects
Bhajananda
Avatar Bhajans
Puja/Arati Hymns
Wingspan
Music from the Matrix I
Music from the Matrix II
Waters of Life
Ever Free Never Bound
Tiger's Paw
Sound Castles
Worlds Unseen
Ecstatic Songs of Ramprasad I
Ecstatic Songs of Ramprasad II

Available at www.SRV.org
And your favorite streaming service.

Advaita-satya-amritam

NECTAR

Of Non-Dual Truth

Subscription Form

Order Next Issue by Mar 25, 2025

Annual Subscription: $18 (U.S.)
Nectar is mailed out once each year in the Spring

Subscribe online: www.srv.org > Nectar Journal > Subscribe
Scan this QR code and you will be right there!

Or, Subscribe by check:

Please fill out the back side of this form and mail it with your check to:
SRV Associations, PO Box 1364, Honokaa, HI 96727 (*payable to: SRV Associations*)

MasterCard or Visa accepted via phone as well:
808-990-3354 ● srvinfo@srv.org ● www.srv.org

#39

Advaita-satya-amritam

NECTAR

Of Non-Dual Truth

Subscription Form

Order Next Issue by Mar 25, 2025

Annual Subscription: $18 (U.S.)
Nectar is mailed out once each year in the Spring

Subscribe online: www.srv.org > Nectar Journal > Subscribe
Scan this QR code and you will be right there!

Or, Subscribe by check:

Please fill out the back side of this form and mail it with your check to:
SRV Associations, PO Box 1364, Honokaa, HI 96727 (*payable to: SRV Associations*)

MasterCard or Visa accepted via phone as well:
808-990-3354 ● srvinfo@srv.org ● www.srv.org

#39

Advaita-satya-amritam

NECTAR

Of Non-Dual Truth

Subscription Form

Order Next Issue by Mar 25, 2025

Annual Subscription: $18 (U.S.)
Nectar is mailed out once each year in the Spring

Subscribe online: www.srv.org > Nectar Journal > Subscribe
Scan this QR code and you will be right there!

Or, Subscribe by check:

Please fill out the back side of this form and mail it with your check to:
SRV Associations, PO Box 1364, Honokaa, HI 96727 (*payable to: SRV Associations*)

MasterCard or Visa accepted via phone as well:
808-990-3354 ● srvinfo@srv.org ● www.srv.org

#39

Your Shipping information: (if subscribing by mail)

Name: _____

Address: _____

City, State, Zip: _____

Email: _____

You Can Help Others Receive Nectar.   Your gift is tax-deductible.

We continue to supply free copies to prison inmates, religious organizations, and persons requiring financial assistance. You can help bridge the financial gap with a separate donation to Nectar. You will receive both our sincere gratitude and a donation letter for your taxes. SRV Associations is a 501c3 tax exempt religious organization.

MasterCard or Visa accepted online at www.srv.org > Giving
Or you can pay by credit card over the phone.
808-990-3354 • srvinfo@srv.org • www.srv.org • Questions? Call or write us!

Your Shipping information: (if subscribing by mail)

Name: _____

Address: _____

City, State, Zip: _____

Email: _____

You Can Help Others Receive Nectar.   Your gift is tax-deductible.

We continue to supply free copies to prison inmates, religious organizations, and persons requiring financial assistance. You can help bridge the financial gap with a separate donation to Nectar. You will receive both our sincere gratitude and a donation letter for your taxes. SRV Associations is a 501c3 tax exempt religious organization.

MasterCard or Visa accepted online at www.srv.org > Giving
Or you can pay by credit card over the phone.
808-990-3354 • srvinfo@srv.org • www.srv.org • Questions? Call or write us!

Your Shipping information: (if subscribing by mail)

Name: _____

Address: _____

City, State, Zip: _____

Email: _____

You Can Help Others Receive Nectar.   Your gift is tax-deductible.

We continue to supply free copies to prison inmates, religious organizations, and persons requiring financial assistance. You can help bridge the financial gap with a separate donation to Nectar. You will receive both our sincere gratitude and a donation letter for your taxes. SRV Associations is a 501c3 tax exempt religious organization.

MasterCard or Visa accepted online at www.srv.org > Giving
Or you can pay by credit card over the phone.
808-990-3354 • srvinfo@srv.org • www.srv.org • Questions? Call or write us!